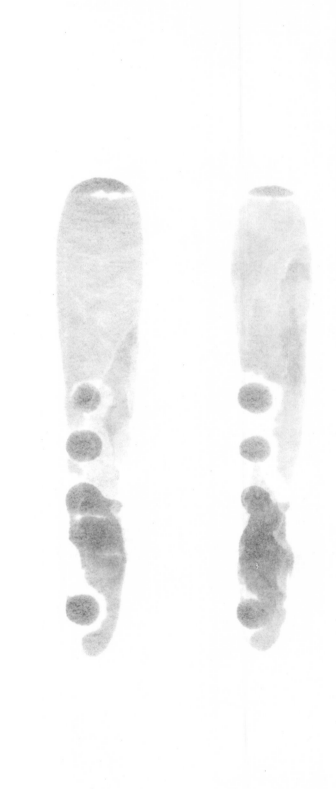

MAKEPEACE

MAKE

A Spirit

PEACE

of Adventure
in Craft & Design

Jeremy Myerson

CONRAN OCTOPUS

First published in 1995 by
Conran Octopus Limited
37 Shelton Street
London WC2H 9HN

Art Editor Pep Sala
Project Editor Denny Hemming
Copy Editor Wendy Dallas
Assistant Editor Jane Chapman
Special Photography Ken Adlard
Picture Research Helen Fickling
Production Controller Julia Golding
Indexer Hilary Bird

British Library Cataloguing-in-Publication Data.

A catalogue record for this book is available from the British Library.

ISBN 1 85029 712 6

Jacket photographs
Front: *Obelisk*. John Makepeace (property of John Makepeace, photography by Jonathan Lovekin)
Back: *Millennium Chair*. John Makepeace (property of The Art Institute of Chicago, photography by Farquharson & Murless)

Typeset in Monotype Modern Extended

Printed and bound in Hong Kong

Contents

The artefacts of sensual beauty and quality which are created in the furniture studio of the English designer John Makepeace do more than just display the special talents of an individual master craftsman. They reflect the artistry and values of an entire creative community.

The base for his activities is Parnham House, a magnificent sixteenth-century Dorset manor house and gardens. It is from here, in a continuing programme of restoration and exploration, that Makepeace directs a wide range of integrated activities in design, craftsmanship, manufacture, ecology, education and woodland management.

The sum of these disciplines reflects a unique vision, which was shaped by a series of early discoveries about the nature of craft, design, architecture and entrepreneurship and is sustained by the spirit of adventure that pervades every aspect of Makepeace's work.

Above: *John Makepeace takes a lead –*
with a walking stick in laminated holly which
literally grabs you by the hand.

Previous page: *Web Table on show in Parnham*
House. This strikingly contemporary piece, made
of maple, burr elm and olive ash in the Makepeace
Studio workshop, adorns ancient halls dating back
to Tudor times.

'My life has been a series of discoveries, of revelations, and continues to be so', says John Makepeace. His contrasting qualities of skill in furniture making and dynamic business acumen are very rarely combined in the area of craft and design, where the most visionary artists and designers are often those who are the furthest removed from the demands of the real world and the least motivated to respond to its ever-changing challenges.

Makepeace is a powerful exception. In many ways he is a man and furniture maker of continual contradiction, who revels in taking seemingly disparate elements and making them part of a single holistic vision. Parnham, which dates back to Tudor times, is now a showcase for contemporary design pieces representing audacious new ways with form and materials. A rural retreat from industry, it is also a setting for research into resources and methods of manufacture to match the needs of the twenty-first century. It houses a studio of international importance for serious furniture collectors yet it also shelters under its wing a school in which young designers take their faltering first steps and artists must learn to be entrepreneurs. Private artistic preoccupations are given a wider public platform by opening the studio workshop, as well as the house and extensive gardens, at Parnham to visitors.

In every facet of Makepeace's work a knowledge of history and a respect for tradition are transcended by the drive to innovate. Nothing demonstrates this better than his pioneering moves to establish a second creative community four miles from Parnham House – in the woodlands of Hooke Park – a centre for research, design, furniture making, education and the management of renewable forest resources. In Makepeace, artistry with precious materials goes hand in hand with a concern for the least valued timber from the forest.

He is never satisfied and never stops moving on to the next challenge. Informed by an immense self-belief and sense of destiny, he brings a restless energy to each new task in a way which is seemingly at odds with the rural serenity of his surroundings. The contradictory forces that motivate him are, however, sometimes hard for outsiders to understand. Makepeace inspires great loyalty among the close-knit community of more than forty people at Parnham, where craftsmen, apprentices, tutors, students and administrators live and work together in a setting akin to a late twentieth-century version of a medieval craft guild. But he is also widely misinterpreted and a target for envy, even resentment, on occasions, especially among those who feel uncomfortable with his decidedly radical approach to the crafts.

Craftsmen are supposed to toil away in glorious poverty in a rural backwater with artistic satisfaction their main reward; they are not supposed to assume the role of lord of the manor, implausibly installed in a country seat while basking in the spotlight of publicity on the international stage. Nor are they supposed to command high prices for their work or build a business enterprise of sufficient momentum to engage modern marketing techniques normally regarded as the exclusive province of industry. Craftsmen may teach the odd apprentice how to make a decent dovetail, but they are certainly not allowed to challenge the status quo in British art and design education – a system still rooted in the moralistic principles of the Bauhaus – and establish a privately funded residential school for young designer-makers whose curriculum stresses the development of entrepreneurial skills. Craftsmen are supposed to be specialists at the micro level, concentrating on the minutest detail or grain; they are not supposed to lift their heads from their work bench to discuss macro-economics or the warp and weave of global construction and manufacturing techniques. Still less should furniture makers challenge prevailing methods in the mother profession of architecture.

Makepeace has done all of these things. Along the way, as his interests have taken him into new, seemingly distracting areas of activity, the furniture designs at the core of his career have continued to express the sensitivity of a master of his craft, and, importantly, to stretch the boundaries of function and structure.

It seems that Makepeace, the self-made designer and entrepreneur, has been able to have his cake and eat it. The fact that he has reinvented himself at different stages of his career has often baffled those who like to pigeonhole people, and who cannot see that the disparate parts of his life form the whole man. What nobody doubts, however, is that he has given the crafts a new relevance in a highly technological age, making fresh, unforeseen connections in a direct and totally uncompromising manner.

Makepeace recognizes the radical impulse of his work and acknowledges that he constantly raises his head above the parapet as an invitation to be shot down. But, guided by a series of highly personal revelations, he has never considered any other stance. 'I see myself as an outsider. I have had to do things in a cavalier way', he explains. 'I don't accept the conventions because they have often been based on the wrong assumptions.'

This book sets out to explore the many contradictory facets of John Makepeace. It looks at his personal background and early rise to prominence as a maker of fine furniture. It reveals his practical and philosophical approaches to his craft, and the relationship of his work to architecture, education and ecology. It also examines his role as the restorer of a grand stately home, the founder of a residential school for craftsmen and the visionary behind new timber construction and manufacturing techniques at Hooke Park. In conclusion, it explores Makepeace's views and beliefs on future patterns of living and working as we approach the new millennium.

Right: *Desert Island Chair carved in elm, 1980, set on a needle-pile rug made by Caroline Slinger. The design, which explores the idea of a mythical island that enables the user to relax with nature, reflects the radical impulse in Makepeace's work.*

John Makepeace's early life provides some important clues to his self-determination and sense of mission. He was born in July 1939 at Solihull in Warwickshire, the fifth and youngest child of a successful Midlands car trader. Christened John Makepeace Smith, in his early twenties he was to adopt his maternal grandmother's maiden name of Makepeace as his surname. His father, 'Tiger' Smith, was president of the Society of Motor Manufacturers and Traders, a tenacious and irascible man, and a Victorian disciplinarian from whom Makepeace clearly inherited an unswerving firmness of purpose. His mother, Marjorie, was the softer, more yielding parent, whose artistic inclinations would later lead her to support him in his chosen career. There are two elder sisters and two elder brothers. It was not, says John Makepeace, a close-knit family. His upbringing was a largely solitary one which, he says, helped him to develop a keen sense of his environment from an early age.

The Smiths evacuated during the war to the North Wales coastal resort of Aberdovey but Makepeace remembers little of that time. His earliest recollections date from 1947, when the family returned to their Warwickshire home, an Edwardian house called Fairfield in Olton, with its extensive garden, a tennis court and a glass conservatory. Two years later his parents bought the Woad House in Fenny Compton, a restored fifteenth-century priory with beautiful gardens, barns and outhouses. Both these properties had a profound influence on the young boy as he grew up, especially in giving him an appreciation of textures and surfaces. Fairfield was unspoilt Edwardiana, and in its well integrated spaces and tiled floors it had a quality of design resolution typical of houses of the period. The Woad House was very different in character: in a glorious setting by a stream deep in the countryside, it had low, beamed ceilings and small windows with lead lights.

It was at Fairfield, with its rotting joinery, that John Makepeace first studied a carpenter at work, and it was there that he became familiar with the furniture made by his paternal grandfather, an Ipswich timber merchant and cabinet maker. His grandfather died before Makepeace was born, but his work helped to kindle the young boy's interest in woodworking; he began taking Saturday carpentry classes at prep school. Already, by the age of six, he had made a boat by hollowing out a piece of wood with a penknife, although as a child he admits he had a reputation for destroying objects rather than making them. 'I had a compulsive desire to understand how things were made', he recalls. 'Perhaps that's why I took them apart.'

Makepeace went to a highly disciplinary prep school at Eversfield in Solihull, an experience he found largely vacuous and sterile. At school, he was an agitated and rebellious pupil, often getting into trouble. He was also a loner, prone to being bullied, whose siblings were already leaving home. The various elements of his education appeared unrelated: 'There was never any joy in academic study', he says.

'I couldn't see the connections. Everything was simply done out of a sense of duty.'

Some things did capture his imagination, however. Makepeace regularly passed the Quaiffe & Lilley cricket bat works adjacent to the canal in Olton. This workshop made bats for the Warwickshire team and others in a series of wooden sheds. After peering into the place nervously on several occasions, he was eventually invited in, shown round and sent home with his own piece of wood. Makepeace remembers it as a significant event in his childhood.

Prep school also kindled an interest in religion. On Sundays the boarders would cycle five miles through coun-

try lanes to church, and in the evening they sang hymns at the home of the headmaster, the Reverend Peacock. The countryside, whose forms are visible in so much of his furniture, was already beginning to exert a strong influence on John Makepeace as a boy. He recalls visiting the farm of his uncle, an expert horseman, and being greatly impressed by his uncle's performance on horseback. In many ways his childhood belonged to a green England that no longer exists – and one which the craft community at Parnham in some way echoes.

Makepeace's first encounter with a professional craftsman was in 1950, at the age of eleven. He went with his mother to see the furniture maker Hugh Burkett, who

Woad House, a restored fifteenth-century priory deep in the English countryside. This family home influenced Makepeace as he was growing up. On the far left is his first workshop; he designed and made the oak and elm fence himself as a summer project.

worked in a recognizably Arts and Crafts style in a workshop at Lapworth near Birmingham. The purpose of the visit was to commission a gift to his father from the Motor Agents' Association. Burkett was highly accomplished, having trained with Oliver Morrell, a latter-day practitioner in the Arts and Crafts Movement, who worked in the Black Mountains in Wales. To see wood worked with such skill to produce objects of uncompromising quality was a profound revelation for Makepeace (although his family never commissioned Burkett and bought instead 'a grotesque Victorian reproduction'). The visit to Burkett's workshop built on his earlier experiences of seeing carpenters at work at Fairfield, taking woodworking lessons and visiting the cricket bat factory at Olton: a seed was sown which would slowly flower.

Makepeace can remember building a wooden bird house for a neighbour at the age of twelve, and around that time he was also commissioned by the local doctor to make a stethoscope case. His first major design-making project came two years later, when his father asked him to build a fence at the family home at the Woad House. Over the summer holiday of 1953 Makepeace planned, designed and costed the job. He did all the work himself, from obtaining quotes from sawmills and buying twenty-one gross of brass screws to digging holes and concreting in the posts. The project went like clockwork and was immensely fulfilling.

In 1952, at the age of thirteen, Makepeace had been sent as a boarder to Denstone College in Staffordshire, which placed strong emphasis on sport and religion. His sense of isolation and anxiety, and of his role as victim, continued. As a relief from the customary bullying by senior pupils and the torture of cross-country runs, he spent time in the school carpenter's workshop. And in 1954 Makepeace was commissioned to make some library shelves for the school by his housemaster at Denstone.

There was no practical design work in the curriculum, no art teaching and virtually no poetry. The only artistic outlet was theatre and he took part in school plays, although he was always happier to be involved in stage management than performing. His only real commitment, supported strongly by the school, was to religion, and from an early stage at Denstone the Church appeared to be a logical career route. 'I felt I could make a contribution. I wasn't ambitious in any material sense and I cared about the world', says Makepeace. 'I was not even attracted to the formalities of religion. What appealed to me was its spirituality.' Indeed, in later life Makepeace was to reject what he describes as the 'trappings and dogma of religion' while retaining and distilling many of its spiritual values.

His father, who had been ill over a period of several years, wanted him to go to Oxford or Cambridge, a benchmark for success that was consistent with his fierce but sometimes insensitive ambitions for his son. Having eventually passed his 'O' level Latin exam, Makepeace studied English, French and European History at 'A' level with the intention of applying for entry to Keble College, Oxford. School reports described him as industrious, as having a sense of duty but lacking enthusiasm. He had doubts about going to university but no alternative to the Church was ever discussed. Then, in April 1957, his father died, which released in him conflicting emotions of bewilderment, grief and liberation. 'My father's death changed the pattern of my life', says Makepeace. 'I had felt pressured and unable to express what I really wanted to do. But now I immediately said no to the Church and no to university. I wanted to make furniture. Of course, I didn't know then how I'd do it or where I'd learn.'

Right: *Circular garden bench, made of teak in eight sections. The piece sits today in an American garden overlooking Lake Michigan.*

John Makepeace's commitment to the crafts, to a radical change in direction, was helped in no small measure by a family friend, Jim Bramley, the export director of the Austin motor car company and later of British Leyland. Bramley was a cosmopolitan, well-travelled character who owned Modernist chairs designed by Bauhaus architect and furniture designer Marcel Breuer. He had recognized the artistic leanings in Makepeace and became a mentor, encouraging the teenager's interest in design matters. On one occasion Bramley arranged to meet Makepeace in the pretty town of Amersfoort in Holland – venue for an Austin promotion – to show him examples of well-designed modern artefacts representative of a progressive society that valued what it produced; they made an immediate impact on the impressionable if independent-minded youngster.

After the death of 'Tiger' Smith, Bramley became a 'substitute father' of sorts for John Makepeace. He introduced him to his neighbours, who lived in a real, solid oak Arts and Crafts house: the blacksmith Alan Knight and his wife, a glass engraver and relation of the designer Edward Barnsley. Knight invited Makepeace to stay overnight and lent him a copy of a limited edition book by Ernest Gimson, an associate of Edward Barnsley's father and uncle, Sidney and Ernest Barnsley. Gimson and the Barnsleys were all well-established artist-craftsmen and important furniture designers within the Arts and Crafts tradition, and the book stimulated in Makepeace an interest in the movement which has never abated. He travelled to London to visit the Craft Centre of Great Britain at Hay Hill, showcase for a wide and coherent range of crafts from furniture and textiles to calligraphy and bookbinding. He saw the work of Edward Barnsley there and was greatly inspired.

Barnsley himself entertained the young Makepeace, advising him that there was no future in furniture making and that he should go into industry instead. Makepeace was already far too set on his course to accept this advice, however, and continued his quest. He sought an apprenticeship at the famous workshops in Broadway, Worcestershire, of Sir Gordon Russell, a self-taught artist-craftsman who had embraced industrial production without abandoning the traditional skills of the cabinet maker. Makepeace admired Russell's achievements and was eager to learn from him but

was told that at eighteen he was already too old to be taken on as an apprentice in his workshop. During that summer of 1957 he followed up other Arts and Crafts leads in the Cotswolds and was introduced to Harry Davol, the only surviving cabinet maker from Sidney Barnsley's workshop. Here was a direct line of communication with the Arts and Crafts Movement. Davol, who lived in a cottage full of his own furniture, added another piece to Makepeace's mental jigsaw of the world the Barnsleys had inhabited.

Supported throughout by his mother, Makepeace pursued his new goal with the relentless vigour that would later be a characteristic trait. Thoughts of a career in the Church had faded fast. 'I was simply driven. There was no way back or out', says Makepeace. 'Craft and making was my new morality. To find something so complete that I could believe in was a wonderful discovery. There appeared to be scope for total involvement and the fulfilment of all the personal needs I perceived at the time.'

Eventually he secured the apprenticeship he was searching for – with the Dorset-based furniture designer and maker Keith Cooper, who agreed to take him on for two years at £2 a week. Makepeace moved into freezing digs in a council house with a single paraffin heater in his room, and began his training. From the start he loved the atmosphere of the workshop and made rapid progress, despite the long hours and arduous work. Many jobs, such as restoring a large, round-topped oak door, involved backbreaking labour. But he felt he had found his vocation. Cooper was a former solicitor who, like many artisans and others before him, adopted the practice of the legal profession, in which an articled clerk paid his employer while learning his trade, and applied it to the crafts. He was a remote tutor, but for Makepeace the simple experience of being in a furniture workshop and not in school was enough.

Keith Cooper was a good maker working within the emerging aesthetics of industrial design, and he had a keen sense of quality. He emphasized practical skills, and encouraged Makepeace to make a drawing desk for entry in a Dorset Art and Craft Competition. The desk, which held a T-square in position by use of magnets, won first prize. However, Cooper advised him early on that he would never make a living as a furniture maker and that he should train by correspondence course to be a handicraft teacher. Makepeace followed this advice, signed up for the course, and in the process made another vital discovery – design. Up until that point he had been inspired by the whole idea of making, of exercising personal will over materials. It did not matter what was being made. The revelation of design as an activity, discussed in detail by the correspondence course, opened his eyes to both the purpose and the potential of what he was doing.

As a child Makepeace had felt disconnected and ill at ease with the world. But now, in Cooper's workshop, he at last began to make connections, to see things as a whole. In particular, he realized that craft making and design were inseparable. The year before, in 1956, the Design Centre had been opened in London by Design Council director Sir Gordon Russell, and the artefacts Makepeace saw there fully endorsed this realization. *Design* magazine, another Russell initiative, had been launched in 1949 and he became an avid reader.

The correspondence course taught the history of furniture, in particular the evolution of structure and form that would later draw Makepeace into the orbit of architecture. It also introduced him to the writings of William Morris, polemical figurehead of the Arts and Crafts Movement, who proved to be another powerful influence: 'I was reacting against my family background in industry. I wanted to do something different. So the anti-industrial stance of the Arts and Crafts struck a positive chord. Here was a set of values within which I could operate.' For the same reasons, the presence in the correspondence course of the design-as-visual-science ethos of the post-1925 Dessau Bauhaus – the German art school which, under director Walter Gropius, moved from exploring art and craft to exploring art and technology – interested him much less.

The strong theoretical approach of his studies provided Makepeace with the perfect counterbalance to the firm, practical grounding in woodworking techniques and skills offered by Keith Cooper's workshop. The foreman there, Brian Wright, who later became the head of woodworking at Bryanston School, answered his many questions and created an environment that was dedicated to the production of high quality work.

The young Makepeace drove across to Scandinavia in an old van to visit the fine furniture workshops preparing artefacts for the annual Copenhagen Cabinet Makers Exhibition. There he saw work by the great contemporary Danish designers including Rasmussen and Finn Juhl. Exposure to such individually crafted pieces at a stage in the late 1950s when industrial design threatened the existence of traditional workshops profoundly influenced his ideas. 'It was the first time I had seen cabinet making which was both aesthetically exciting and technically innovative', Makepeace recalls.

Right: *Detail from a desk made for a Dorset farming family using local but unusual materials. The set of pigeonholes on the desk-top has drawer fronts in oysters of laburnum and an end grain of pseudo-acacia. Makepeace's discovery of craft skills and natural materials was initially a reaction against his family background in industry.*

resonant for Makepeace throughout his career. Ruskin's famous saying 'Art without industry is guilt, industry without art is brutality', mirrored precisely the dilemma that Makepeace, as the young craft apprentice escaping from an industrial family background, was seeking to understand.

He began to focus on the relationship between hand and machine techniques; both were employed in Keith Cooper's workshop and they sat awkwardly together. Handmaking techniques encouraged one aesthetic, machine methods another. In any case, there would surely be no market for batch-produced objects made by hand in small numbers, as in Cooper's workshop, if they could be made more swiftly and inexpensively by machine. 'If a piece was handmade, then it needed to say something about the individual maker, the process involved and the circumstances in which it was created', comments Makepeace.

Towards the end of his two-year apprenticeship he became restlessly eager to put some of his newly developed ideas into practice. He had mastered many techniques and was already productive as a maker. He wanted to set up his own workshop, but first he needed to carry out two years' handicraft teaching in order to complete his qualification. Between 1959 and 1961 he worked in Birmingham as a teacher, first in a school in the tough, inner-city area of Small Heath where some children had no shoes or shirts, and then in the somewhat better social conditions of Sparkbrook. Though this experience made an incongruous precursor to Makepeace's later role as the founder of a private design school, it nevertheless opened his eyes to what he describes as 'society in the raw'. He comments 'I was never a natural teacher but I gained a good understanding of how people learn'.

His family had sold the Woad House in 1957 and his mother had gone to look after his brother Derek, a farmer, on a 500-acre (202-ha) farm in Warwickshire. Makepeace's home was now the farmhouse, Hodnell Manor, and it was here that he returned each weekend from teaching in Birmingham. He converted a wagon shed into a makeshift workshop and began making pieces to order. By 1959, when he moved his workshop to a dairy on the farm, his business was already building nicely. Among his early commissions at Hodnell Manor was a desk for his brother in lieu of rent.

A piece in yew entitled Desk With A View, dating from 1970. The writing surfaces contain pencil drawers which slide forward to hold stationery.

Makepeace qualified as a teacher but never saw the profession as a future career. He was determined not to fail as a designer-maker. He was accepted via selection of work (which included a chest of drawers and a giant columnar light) as a member both of the Craft Centre of Great Britain, the leading craft body of the time, based in London, and of its northern equivalent, the Red Rose Guild in Manchester, which exhibited annually at the prestigious Whitworth Art Gallery. For one so young to win this recognition as a craftsman was exceptional.

Makepeace designed all his own early pieces, among them bookshelves, lamps and a nest of tables. He even employed his own apprentice, a fourteen-year-old by the name of John Bunford. Today, more than thirty years later, Bunford works with him on the construction of the buildings at Hooke Park, after a varied career in teaching, shopfitting and industry. This is an illustration of the lines of continuity that run through John Makepeace's career.

In 1961, at the age of twenty-two, Makepeace made his first trip to North America, which proved to be another eye-opener. 'There appeared to be infinite choice and freedom. It taught me that anything is possible', he says. He took a job for one month in Austin Leyland's Toronto office, then delivered a car to Vancouver, and proceeded from there on a marathon tour of the United States by Greyhound bus. En route he visited leading designers, showrooms and retailers. Nobody slammed a door in his face. Everybody, from California to New York, welcomed him. Many of the department stores and speciality shops sold objects of exceptional quality, and he found the positive atmosphere invigorating; as Makepeace recalls, the New World offered a distinct contrast to stuffy old class-ridden Britain, which was still emerging slowly from an era of austerity.

One episode clouded the rosy glow: Makepeace, a fastidious timekeeper, had an appointment in Dallas with Stanley Marcus, founder of the Neiman Marcus retail chain. But he overslept in his hotel; exhausted after two days' continuous travelling, unshaven and distracted by losing his luggage, he uncharacteristically stood up one of America's most powerful arbiters of contemporary taste.

It was during his travels in America that he resolved to change his surname from Smith to Makepeace, which reflected his Quaker family connections. He toyed briefly with the name John Makepeace Smith but preferred the simpler form. Makepeace it was. 'I felt curiously liberated by the decision. It was another escape from my father's influence.'

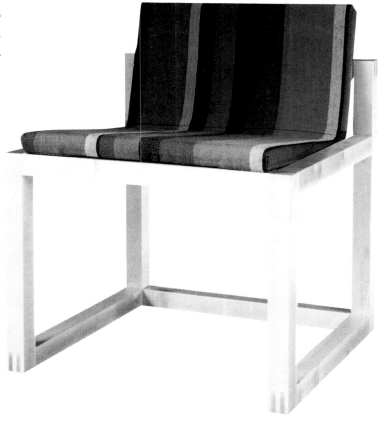

Dining chair in sycamore with cotton upholstery, 1964. It was designed by Makepeace as part of a range for series production and reflected the new Habitat-inspired industrial look of the period. However, its maker would later draw back from volume production for retail markets to explore a more expressive and consciously craft-based aesthetic.

Life at Hodnell Manor in the early Sixties took on its own momentum. Orders began to flow in from the Craft Centre of Great Britain and the Red Rose Guild, and Makepeace exhibited at craft shows in Birmingham and Stoneleigh. A member of the local landed gentry, Sir Charles Shuckburgh, commissioned some display cabinets and there was also more mundane work on offer, such as name-plates, letter cutting and antique restoration. Makepeace, eager to make his own designs, loathed restoring antiques but needed to ensure the survival of his fledgling venture.

He soon began to establish connections with other designer-craftsmen, and in 1962 he organized an exhibition at the Herbert Art Gallery in Coventry of the work of twelve notable designers. They included the blacksmith Alan Knight, who had given him such vital early encouragement, the bookbinder Ivor Robinson, silversmith Robert Welch and textile makers Peter Collingwood and Ann Sutton. The innovative constructed textiles of Ann Sutton particularly caught Makepeace's eye. She shared his interest in exploring new structural forms in design, and their partnership blossomed on both a professional and a personal level. They were married in 1964.

John Makepeace saw his base at Hodnell Manor as an interim arrangement. He badly wanted his own workshop-showroom, with easy access for customers, and began the search for a new location. Ideally, he wanted to move to the Cotswolds. The Blenheim Estate offered him a beautiful old mill rent-free, but the deal involved an enormous amount of building restoration and Makepeace felt disinclined to spend the rest of his life renovating someone else's property. Alternatives, including a shop, workshop and house in the town of Woodstock, and a workshop and barn offered by a landowner nearby, also hit snags. It was hard to get planning permission for noisy workshops in the picturesque English villages where Makepeace wanted to live and work.

Eventually he found a solution just five miles from his brother's farm. Farnborough Barn was an isolated, 33-acre (13-ha) site with derelict farm buildings visible from the Coventry-Banbury road. The local planning officer assured him that an application to put furniture workshops on the

Below: *A muddy, derelict Farnborough Barn before restoration by Makepeace in the early 1960s.*

Bottom: *After the renovation a creative community takes shape, complete with Swiss chalet-style living accommodation.*

site would be looked upon favourably, and Makepeace bid for the property at auction; he acquired his first craft home for £5,000. With money inherited from his father and a bank loan, he then converted the cow shed on the site into a workshop and spent the next twelve months living there while he converted the barn into a house.

In retrospect, Makepeace concedes that his first architectural experiment was only partially successful. He built his own modern home at Farnborough Barn but confessed later that he felt it was an aesthetic compromise. 'The site was bold, isolated, in open country. It was ideal for a sculptural statement', he recalls, 'but I chose the wrong architect and I didn't have the confidence at the time to argue with him or the planners.' Makepeace was anxious not to have planning permission refused because of the cost implications so he gave in to the Scandinavian design ideas which were becoming fashionable at the time. His chalet-style home was a competent enough construction project – its sloping roof was tiled with split cedar 'shakes', only the second building in the United Kingdom to use them – but he was never really happy with what its design symbolized. Always his own sternest critic, Makepeace saw its form as a reflection of his initial lack of courage in commissioning architecture, and the experience taught him a lesson about architects and planners that he would put to good use in future encounters on the building site.

For several months he energetically organized sub-contractors – bricklayers, electricians, plumbers – at Farnborough Barn, while doing all the carpentry, joinery and roofing work himself. He also worked as a bricklayer's labourer and undertook some of the messiest jobs on the site, such as digging out the chicken pens full of flea-ridden manure. The results were rewarding but it was the second architectural commission there – the conversion of a wagon shed into a craft gallery by architect Graham Anthony – that gave him the greatest pleasure: 'It was my first involvement in an architectural commission which graduated from controlling construction to architecture as an art.' One building was turned into a shop, with a weaving studio above it for Ann Sutton (and was to become a housekeeper's cottage when Ann moved her textile studio into the house). At last all the pieces of the jigsaw were in place.

Left: *Leather-stitched chair built on a steel armature, dating from the early 1970s. Its approach shows the influence of Joe Columbo, the radical Sixties Italian designer, in the way legs and upholstery are integrated to create a soft form.*

Below: *Clover Leaf storage unit in birch ply and acrylic on a stainless steel column, purchased by the Victoria & Albert Museum, London.*

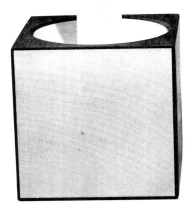 

The Ionic range of desk and shelf accessories in sycamore and rosewood veneer represented Makepeace's most sustained and successful attempt in the mid-1960s to develop a collection of products for the retail trade.

While initial building work was under way at Farnborough Barn Makepeace won a £600 prize for a circular kitchen design in a competition organized by *The Observer* newspaper. He used the prizemoney to visit Nigeria with Ann: he wanted to study the mud buildings; she wanted to look at two-dimensional patterns on three-dimensional forms. The primitive round African dwellings he encountered had a profound effect on his thinking as a furniture designer at the time. 'The form was entirely logical and appropriate to people gathering to talk and cook', recalls Makepeace. 'I was fascinated by an architecture which so neatly embraced the occupations of daily life. As furniture supports human activity, I began to argue in my work for the rounded shapes I'd seen in those homes in Nigeria.' For one project he created a round desk for a translator working in an attic space, supporting the writing and shelving areas on a circular podium. The idea of softened, rounded, organic shapes, as opposed to the rectilinear, hard-edged approach of the Modern Movement, appealed to Makepeace because such forms were both more comfortable and more efficient to use.

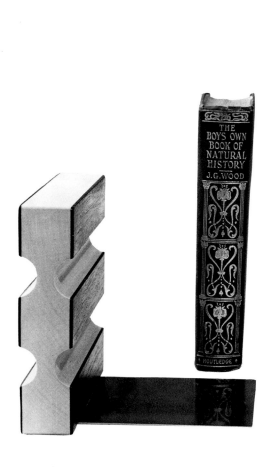

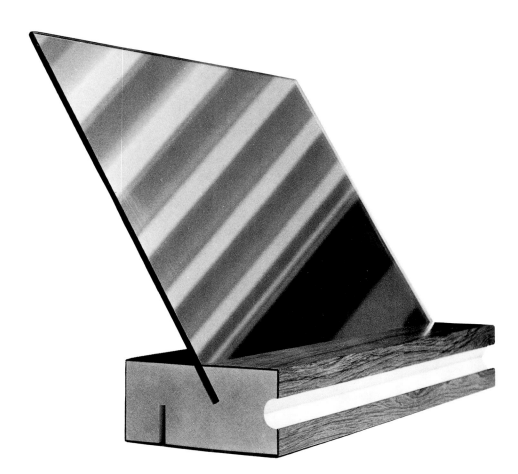

As orders grew, so did Makepeace's enterprise. By now his workshop employed four people. An additional workshop space and timber store was added at the back of the site. In the early Sixties he toyed briefly with the idea of pursuing a fellowship at the Royal College of Art, having met the great craft maker and theorist David Pye who was a professor there, but he decided against it. Nothing – not even an RCA education – was going to deflect him from his urgent desire to make progress in his career.

By the mid-Sixties he had decided that he needed to make retail products in some volume to support his scale of operations. So he developed the Ionic range, which included a set of desk accessories – candle-holders, ashtrays, book ends and so on – wrapping a sycamore core in a rosewood veneer. These sold well in the leading London furniture store Heal's, and some twenty other retailers across England, so more retail designs for batch production were developed, including a glass-topped table made of teak or beech; known in the trade as a knock-down table, it packed flat to form a crate for the glass and was designed to be assembled by the customer using four screws.

Makepeace found himself spending one day a week away from Farnborough Barn as he took on the role of salesman. 'The entrepreneurial side of my career was an entirely intuitive development', he recalls. 'I was driven by my own sense of frustration at what was available at the time.' He was a determined salesman, often persuading retail buyers to stock his product by actually carrying a new chair or table into the store and setting it down on the floor for the public to gather round it. The scale of the retail orders, including one from the Courts furniture retailer for a hundred tables to be delivered to twenty different shops, became daunting. There was plenty of business for the workshop at Farnborough Barn and Makepeace gained national recognition as a designer-maker of quality during the Sixties. Nevertheless he still felt he lacked a coherent focus.

At this point in his life he had still to confront the dichotomy of design versus making. So much of woodworking technique was to do with precision, with the mastery of tools, process and material, that technical skill took precedence over conceptual thinking. Woodworking was so demanding and hard to do well that the mastery of preci-

sion, rather than designing, became the primary focus and reward for craftsmen. 'That explains why so much craft work is derivative rather than original in concept, whilst being well made', says Makepeace. 'In my career, there has been a gradual integration of the technical and conceptual. It took a long time to make a creative statement which communicated with the user of the object and said something about their circumstances as well as those of the craftsman. It was like a child learning basic words and beginning to convey ideas through sentences and then receiving a response. That is what design as communication is all about.'

In the process of learning to speak fluently, Makepeace attempted to master a variety of tongues. In 1965 he produced a range of very simple, modern tables and chairs with plain frames, the tables with white melamine tops. This was shortly after the opening of Terence Conran's shop in Hanway Place, off London's Tottenham Court Road, and utilitarian chic was all the rage. *The Times* devoted a full page to Makepeace's fresh, industrial-looking range and the architectural press, schooled in Bauhaus ideology, praised the work to the skies. But despite all this glowing coverage, not a single piece was sold. The experience was a salutary one: it taught Makepeace a lesson he has never forgotten. 'I discovered that the furniture was more expensive to make than its appearance suggested. It looked like an industrial product even though it was largely handmade. It confirmed my suspicion that I either had to find more economical ways of working in product areas where price is crucial, or create objects totally free from that association.'

The episode marked the beginning of Makepeace's endeavour to devise a more expressive and less rectilinear aesthetic for furniture, one which recognizably reflects the level of work that goes into it. He saw that it was pointless as a craft maker to create pieces with a machine aesthetic, no matter how popular that aesthetic might be at the time. Initially, however, he pursued the two alternative streams simultaneously: special craft commissions for private clients and batch-production of retail lines, such as the successful knock-down table he had made for Heal's. He exploited machine techniques in order to be price-competitive in the mid-1960s, and he could have pursued that industrial route profitably. But he decided to withdraw from it completely.

'I had the opportunity to manufacture in greater volumes', he says, 'but that would have demanded a major capital investment and required me to compete in an already depressed furniture industry; it would also have exposed me to the vagaries of a cyclical retail furniture market. I have always been prepared to take a commercial view on such activities as manufacturing for retailers, property management or opening the house at Parnham to the public. But with my own furniture my priorities are always designing and making because its quality and detail are so personal to me.'

In 1968 he appointed a Manchester Business School graduate, John Jones, as manager of his workshop. This was totally unprecedented in craft circles. Jones, who had gained substantial commercial experience with large multi-national companies, had joined Makepeace in the hope of finding a new direction in his own life. He introduced mainstream management disciplines to the workshop and asked fundamental questions of a small craft set-up which no other furniture maker in the United Kingdom faced. He was interested in the problems of small businesses and he forced Makepeace to confront and try to resolve some of the more unpalatable economic truths concerned with being a designer-maker in a labour-intensive field. Importantly, he made Makepeace write down his aims. The results were revealing. First, Makepeace wanted to make furniture without compromise. Second, he wanted the business to survive. Third, he wanted to achieve personal growth as a designer-maker. Nowhere did he mention building larger markets or achieving wider recognition. 'The exercise revealed to me that there had to be a way of operating that was better than simply growing bigger for its own sake', he recalls. Jones would later become the first business tutor when the school at Parnham was set up.

Left: *Boardroom table and chairs for the Royal Scottish Museum, Edinburgh, in ash with a pink suede-effect fabric. Conservation students as well as senior staff use the gate-legged table, which can be folded over and away to clear the room completely for entertaining.*

An interesting new market opened up for Makepeace in the late 1960s: interior contracts. He relished the idea of working alongside some of the leading architects of the day on new schemes, indulging his fascination with space, structure and interior design.

His first commission of this kind was to design and make all the furniture and fittings for twenty-four study bedrooms at the Oxford Centre for Management Studies (today known as Templeton College). This was being built by architects Ahrends, Burton & Kolarek (ABK) who, nearly twenty years later, would be his first architects at Hooke Park. Makepeace won the commission because a client, for whom he had made a rosewood desk, introduced him to the college's administrator, Bill Impey. The project was a new experience for Makepeace, and he soon realized that furniture was always a poor relation to architecture when budgets and deadlines were tight. The making went well but the building's completion was delayed, and he was forced to store all twenty-four sets of furniture in his own home until it was ready. 'I also found my position at the interface between the precision of furniture and the imprecision of architecture hard to deal with at times', he observes. The Study Centre building was opened by the Duke of Edinburgh in 1968 and, with it, new avenues opened up for John Makepeace.

The director of the Oxford Centre, Norman Leyland, and its founder, Clifford Barclay, took a keen interest in his ideas and became personal friends and mentors. Leyland, an Economics Don at Brasenose College, Oxford, and a leading business academic, was curious that a craftsman should employ a business manager. Barclay, a leading figure at the British Film Institute, a successful entrepreneur and later a governor of the London School of Economics, engaged Makepeace in probing conversations about the economy and the arts. It was Barclay who encouraged him to explain and explore his ideas about how craftsmen should be trained. He also became an enlightened patron, commissioning furniture pieces in a way which gave Makepeace complete autonomy and freedom.

Circular workstation for a translator, reflecting Makepeace's fascination with the rounded shapes of primitive African dwellings. The shelves are of sycamore and smooth vinyl.

Total interiors began to feature heavily in the workshop in the early 1970s. Makepeace again collaborated with ABK, making furniture for 120 students' and fellows' rooms in a new residential building at Keble College, Oxford. He also designed and made furniture for a headmaster's study at Banbury Grammar School, the intimate grouping of elements designed to improve communications with parents, teachers and pupils. It was around this time that he created a study and dressing room for Clifford Barclay.

While commissions for the Oxford Centre and Keble College led to a series of total interior projects for offices, in the early 1970s a spate of commissions from museums, who wished to buy pieces for their permanent collections, reinforced Makepeace's reputation as a designer of individual objects. Birmingham City Art Gallery bought a folding screen, Cardiff City Museum a chest of drawers, and the Fitzwilliam Museum in Cambridge commissioned a large cabinet for their contemporary sculpture gallery. Leeds City Art Gallery acquired a display cabinet and the Victoria & Albert Museum's director, Sir Roy Strong, bought a pivoted cabinet in plywood, acrylic and stainless steel. 'I realized

Total interior schemes from the early 1970s:

Below left: *Corner of a study and dressing room designed by Makepeace for Clifford Barclay, founder of the Oxford Centre for Management Studies, with wardrobes and desking of yew.*

Below right: *One of a series of negotiating desks for a Banbury estate agent, with fabric-upholstered settles and screens supported by the desk.*

that machinery can release or compromise your creative freedom just as much as hand skills, and that ingenuity in making is equally vital to both individual and series-produced objects. I was therefore determined to use machines alongside hand skills where appropriate – even though I remembered people like Edward Barnsley and Bernard Leach standing up at conferences and warning craftsmen not to touch machines.'

Exposure to men of such fine minds as Norman Leyland and Clifford Barclay had made Makepeace focus more intensely on the nature of management in his own endeavours. The result was another major career-forging revelation. 'I discovered that management is creative, like any other discipline, and that creativity is not confined to the arts', says Makepeace. 'I also realized that management skills were absent from the education and training of the very people who needed them most to direct their efforts – professional designer-makers.'

Gradually a new idea began to take shape in his mind. 'I had a vision of a college like the Oxford Centre for Management Studies, but one for craftsmen and designers who would learn design, making and business skills in an integrated educational environment', says Makepeace. The purpose of the Oxford Centre was to enable senior executives from business to reassess their thinking at a key stage in their careers. Could a college for designer-makers attempt a similar task? 'I sounded out the concept on Clifford Barclay. He said it was a good idea and that I should go ahead and do it. I had hoped he'd agree to fund it.'

John Makepeace's interest in educational philosophy stems from his experience of teaching in Birmingham and from his own sterile and unsatisfactory schooling; he had studied without conviction or any sense of joy, and slowly he began to understand that for people to learn they must recognize some need or desire within themselves. He also understood that the earlier you found a purposeful direc-

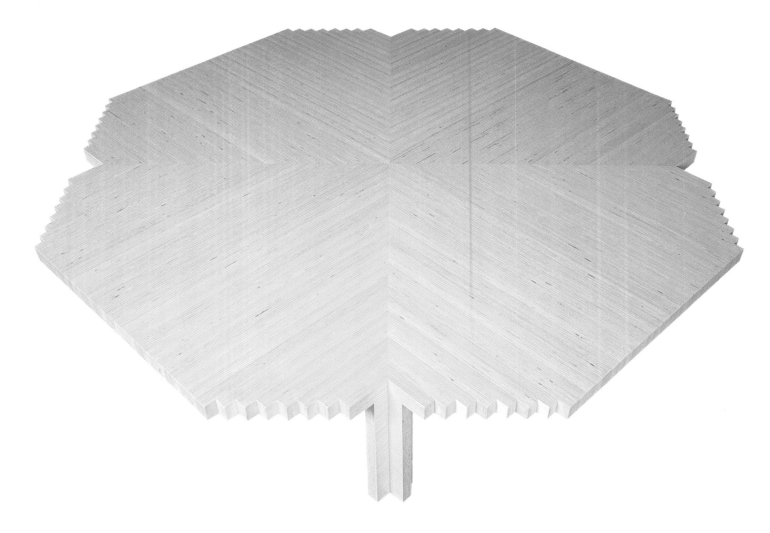

tion, the greater the certainty with which you pursued it. As he explains, 'Later on, as you learn to deal with abstraction of thought, you can easily become ambivalent because you can always think of good arguments as to why you shouldn't do something.' Makepeace further recognized the importance of mentors who take a personal interest in your ideas. He had benefited greatly from the influence of his family friend Jim Bramley. As his broad ideas about the nature of learning took shape, so he began to think about creating an educational vehicle to help young people entering the crafts.

Left: A table dating from the late 1960s. It is made from a series of L-shapes, cut from four pieces of ply, and plays games with the alternating direction in the grain. The piece shows how design ingenuity swiftly underscored technical ability in Makepeace's fast-developing career.

AN EDUCATIONAL CREDO

Makepeace's adventurous decision to press ahead towards the establishment of a new type of private college for craftsmen, incorporating designing, making and entrepreneurship, owed much to the combination of factors that influenced him in the early 1970s.

These included the climate surrounding the setting up of the Crafts Council in 1972, which was established by the Government to improve and promote the work of artist-craftsmen. Makepeace was invited by Lord Eccles, then Minister for the Arts, to become a founder member of this new organization, a state-sector initiative which, ironically, proved to be a catalyst in crystallizing his vision of a private school. Lord Eccles had already visited Farnborough Barn with Lord Reilly, director of the Design Council, and Lord Goodman, chairman of the Arts Council, to discuss the Crafts Council's objectives. Together they established that its key aim would be to support higher creative standards at a time when designs in many aspects of manufacturing, such as woodworking, were seen to be repetitive and derivative.

Makepeace saw the flaws in this idealistic approach, however: 'The Crafts Council was being set up to promote and improve the work of people who didn't exist. I'd searched the UK to find a suitable education and training for myself. There were very few people working in the crafts field and, of those, many were inspired amateurs. I became convinced that none of the existing colleges were run in a way which would attract and train high-calibre people as designer-makers.'

Makepeace was a governor of Rycotewood College, a traditional school in Thame, Oxfordshire, for aspiring craftsmen in wood, as well as a regular guest lecturer at other art, design and technical colleges. On every course he visited he found that the kind of professional and entrepreneurial skills that all fledgling craft makers needed to survive in the real world were absent from the curriculum.

In 1972 Makepeace went to America to discuss a travelling exhibition of his work proposed by the Smithsonian Institute in Washington DC and to visit the leading American furniture designer Wendell Castle. He and Castle

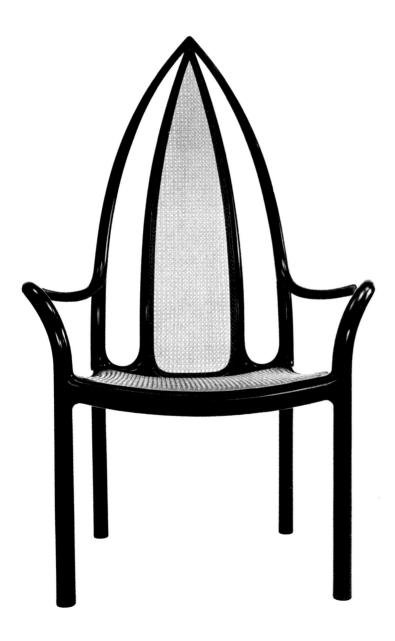

Mitre Chair in ebony and nickel silver, designed and made in 1977 shortly after Makepeace's arrival at Parnham House. Today the chair forms part of a private collection in Oxford.

talked about setting up a design school in New York State and even looked at possible buildings. But events took a different turn.

On Makepeace's return to the United Kingdom, a telegram was waiting from the Rochester Institute of Technology in upstate New York, inviting him to discuss the post of Head of the School of Artisanry. It was a top-notch American appointment, perhaps the educational challenge that he had been looking for. So Makepeace recrossed the Atlantic for an interview. He was destined for disappointment. 'A day at the Institute was enough to convince me that I didn't want to do the job. It was too politically charged', he recalls. 'The Rochester episode was a further catalyst to founding my own school.' Surrounded by educational set-ups which disappointed and depressed him, Makepeace believed he could see what was really needed – a new type of educational venture which was independent of government and local authority controls, and more integrated and focused in terms of disciplines than any he had so far encountered.

He was convinced that political and financial independence was vital in order to develop an educational model free from all enshrined preconceptions about design teaching and learning. The naive letters and portfolios he received every week from art and design graduates seeking work reflected the inadequacy of the available training. A residential school sited right next door to a professional design workshop, taking commissions and dealing with customers, would inject a healthy dose of commercial realism into the course curriculum. In addition, the problems encountered by many technically proficient makers as they struggled to understand the conceptual side of their work indicated to Makepeace the need for a course structure that integrated making and business skills with design.

He saw the liberal, open-ended values of art and design education in the early 1970s as producing graduates without real direction or drive. He wanted to attract students of higher intellectual calibre than training courses in the crafts had hitherto managed to do, convinced that they would be more motivated and entrepreneurial in their approach. They would also be better equipped to make the vital connections between technical expertise, conceptual skill and communication with customers and markets that he knew from experience were needed for craft workshops to survive. Design, making and marketing became the holy trinity of disciplines on which Makepeace began to base his educational credo.

One final factor proved decisive in his drive to found his own school. Makepeace had chosen to keep his workshop small and avoid the major capital investment that an expansion in manufacturing would entail. His aim, successfully achieved, had been quality rather than growth. But now he had surplus energies to expend; he needed to set new personal objectives. He had experienced the need to build self-reliance and self-confidence and wanted to pass that experience on to the next generation of designer-makers.

ACHIEVING A GOAL

In 1975 Liberty & Co, the famous London design and furnishings store, celebrated its centenary and, in the same way as it had commissioned items from leading artists and craftsmen in the early days of its history, Charles Rennie Mackintosh among them, the company commissioned Makepeace to design a dining-room table to mark the event. This was a great honour and Makepeace – by now the best-known furniture maker of his generation in Britain – responded with a stunning *tour de force*: a majestic limed oak table 10 feet (3m) in diameter, comprising four interlocking leaves resting on a carved base. The piece was so huge that it was impossible to assemble it in the workshop; it had to be set up in the gallery. Makepeace saw his struggles with this large-scale project as a sign that he needed to move his entire operation to more spacious premises.

All his early experiences, his influences and instincts told him that only a new creative centre, incorporating on one site a larger workshop, a gallery for display, a residential school for craftsmen and a private home, could encompass the many different facets of his steadily expanding career.

A community of the kind he envisaged – uniting design, making, entrepreneurship, environmental concerns, education and training – would require a special architectural setting to function successfully. Here, Makepeace – an inventive and ambitious renovator of property – began to think of the potential of large, historic houses, many of which were lying empty and in a state of disrepair by the mid-1970s; during the recent period of social change the cost of maintaining them had become too great for their owners to sustain. A number of Makepeace's more prosperous customers and collectors lived in old houses, and some were reluctant to commission adventurous contemporary pieces for fear they would look out of place in traditional domestic surroundings. He saw that, by demonstrating how expressively new furniture could be used in an ancient building, he could encourage patronage of increasingly ambitious experiments in material, structure and form.

He was also very struck by the idea of putting craft education and craft practice – elements which were normally devoid of contact – together at the same location. A number of graduates, mainly from the Royal College of Art, had been employed in his workshop for a period before setting up on their own, and he saw the way they grew in confidence and stature as a result of that experience.

Makepeace's intention from the start was that the entire creative centre should be open to the public. In this way as many people as possible could be invited to share in his ideals and spread the word, as well as supporting students, viewing exhibitions and buying furniture. This aspect of the venture he believed to be an essential part of the goal to which his early discoveries and endeavours had been leading. All these themes were about to be united in one special place: Parnham House in Dorset.

LIBERTY TABLE

The Liberty Table was made by John Makepeace in 1975 to commemorate the centenary of Liberty & Co, the famous London design and furnishings store. Its extraordinary construction is the result of a visually arresting experiment by its maker to create a hollow table top from solid oak.

The limed oak piece is 10 feet (3m) in diameter. It comprises four interlocking, organically-curved leaves sitting on a rugged carved base with the textural characteristic of a mature oak tree; each interface between the leaves is coloured red, green, yellow and blue, creating a satisfying pattern and also representing the four seasons. Makepeace left a void in the centre of the table, a space around which the leaves are joined, so that nobody would be tempted to place a vase of greenery there and so impede conversation.

The centenary commission from Liberty's was a highly prestigious one, given the retailer's unique status in British design and craft. It confirmed Makepeace's arrival as the outstanding designer-maker of his generation. But his struggles in assembling the piece also told him that he had outgrown his Banbury workshop and that he needed to move to somewhere larger. Today the Liberty Table is on public view at Parnham House.

Right: *Liberty Table and matching chairs on display at Parnham House.*

Left: *A chair detail continues the controlled organic theme*

Overleaf: *Surface detail shows the curving relationship of the interlocking leaves.*

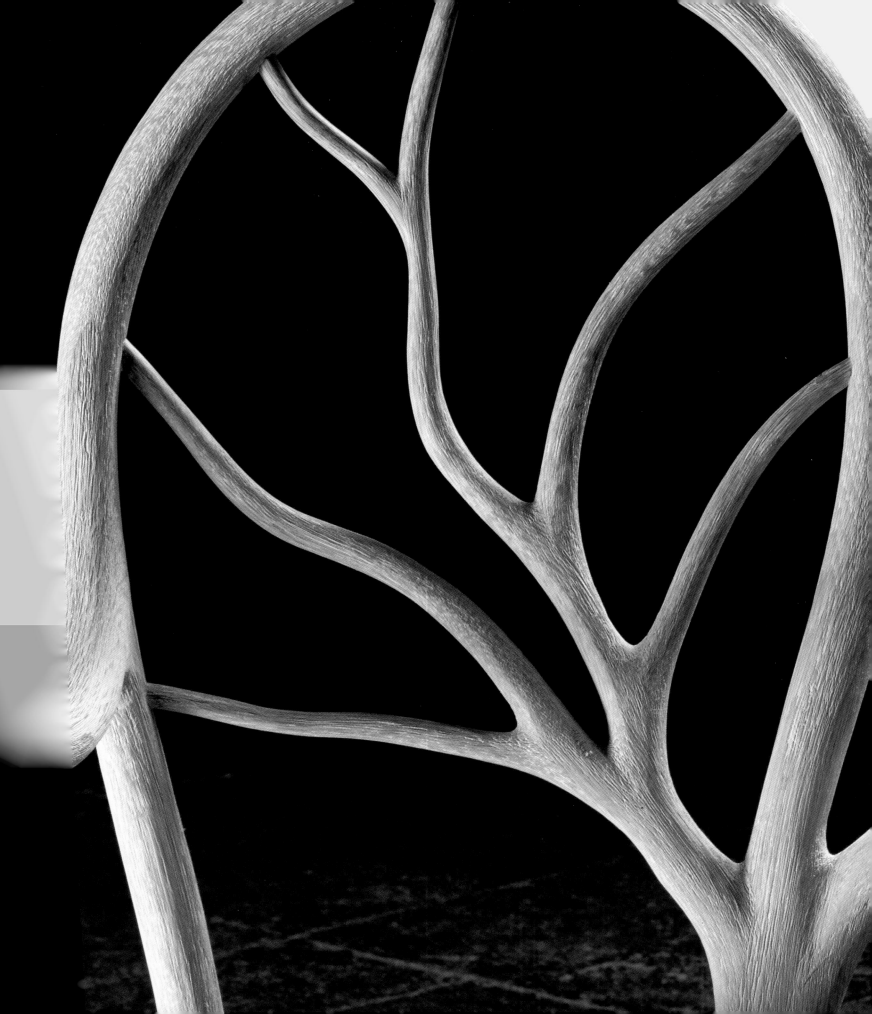

These Sylvan Chairs in laminated oak and leather (previous page and left) were designed and made for a British client who wanted furniture for an informal dining room overlooking a coppice woodland. Makepeace saw in the commission the opportunity to create chairs which would effectively dissolve the boundaries between the interior of the room and the natural woodland outside, and which would induce a sense of ease within the user.

The project reflected Makpeace's belief that people feel more relaxed when surrounded by natural, organic forms rather than by rectilinear, machine-made ones. It also marked his most conscious attempt after the Liberty Table project to use natural forms in his furniture in a very literal way.

A series of six Sylvan Chairs was commissioned, but one was inadvertently made back to front. So a seventh was produced in the Parnham workshop. But this slip-up was destined to have a happy ending: when the client heard of the mistake, he immediately asked to purchase the oddball chair along with the matching six.

This chair in oak and leather was a sequel to the Sylvan Chairs, a present from a mother to her actress daughter.

Left: *Dining-room table and chairs in laminated and scrubbed oak, designed as a deliberate response to the architectural flavour of a home in an early nineteenth-century Edinburgh crescent.*

Overleaf: *A refinement and simplification of the dining table, in cherrywood with wenge veneer top. The triangulating carved leg configuration contacts the ground at four points, not six, forming a stiff, integrated structure with the top. It is a characteristic of Makepeace to rework and develop certain themes from piece to piece.*

Below: *Dining table in oak with a wenge veneer top, designed for a London home with a collection of Art Nouveau furniture. The flowing leg structure, which touches the ground at six points, faintly echoes Art Nouveau patterning in its construction.*

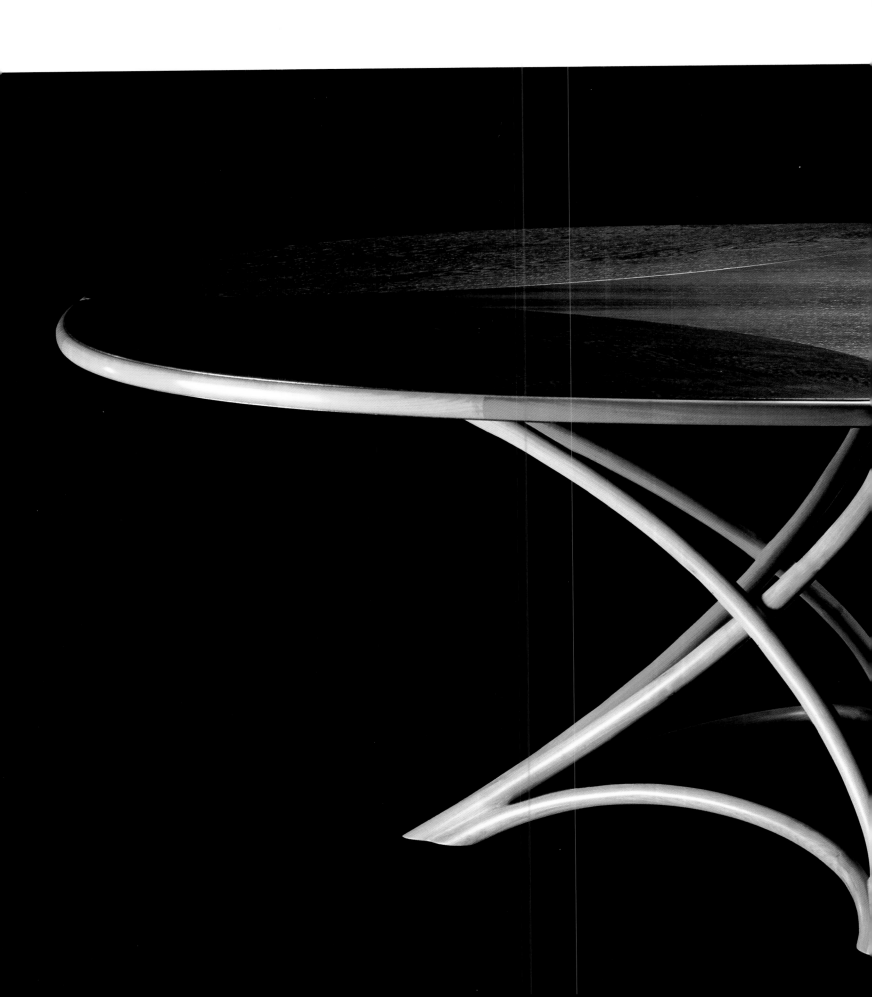

ECLIPSE 2 CABINET

A geometric study in material luxury and mechanical accomplishment, this drinks cabinet has a smooth action which reveals the inner contents upon opening. It is veneered in burr yew with a frame of bog oak and an interior of white English holly, and works on the principle of two pivoted elements: to open, an inner cabinet pivots within the outer shell (see right).

The piece reveals how Makepeace's initial anti-industrial stance, when discovering the romance of the Art and Crafts Movement in his late teens, has given way during his career to a genuine fascination with the principles of engineering and mechanical construction – albeit using unusual materials unassociated with industry.

The development of Parnham House as a self-supporting creative community, and its successful emergence as a place of international repute, marks a key stage in Makepeace's journey of discovery as a designer and maker. The skilful and imaginative restoration of a Plantagenet manor house to provide a setting for a radical new craft venture reflects his message that contemporary design can enhance an ancient building.

At Parnham, Makepeace has not only extended the boundaries of his own work, and made his experiments accessible to the visiting public; but by training a new generation of designer-makers in his residential school he has also stimulated a renaissance in high-quality, craft-based furniture in Britain. Thus Parnham has come to represent not only the home of a master maker but also a fountainhead of new design talent.

Previous page: *Main entrance to Parnham House, a Grade 1 listed historic building rescued from decay and neglect by John Makepeace's determination to create a crafts community within its walls.*

Right: *The North Courtyard, entrance to the Makepeace Furniture Studio.*

In seeking an appropriate setting for the centre, Makepeace initially considered developing the buildings at Farnborough Barn. However, he recognized that they were not of sufficient quality to justify staying there. His Banbury base was already beginning to feel cramped, without adding a school. The hunt for a new home began in the mid-1970s in and around the local area, but nothing suitable could be found so the scope of the search widened. Estate agent John Inge of Knight, Frank & Rutley – later a patron of the Makepeace studio – advised on comparative property prices in different parts of the United Kingdom.

As a result, particulars of five properties further afield were proposed to Makepeace, including one in Dorset, where he had done his apprenticeship. On a fateful, sunny spring day in 1976 he drove down a long, tree-lined drive to Parnham House, a Grade 1 listed Tudor manor house just outside Beaminster. With its grand, mellowed façades and extensive, unkempt gardens, Parnham was a handsome place fallen on hard times. It was owned by the Mental Health Association, MIND, and had most recently been used as a nursing home for 'mentally frail and elderly ladies'. The Great Hall was stacked high with hospital beds, there was linoleum on the floors and fluorescent lighting overhead. The smell of incontinence was everywhere. As a listed building, Parnham had not complied with the fire regulations since to do so would have involved damaging its historic interiors, and in 1973 it had been forced to close as a nursing home. It had been empty for almost three years when Makepeace first inspected it, but he immediately felt that it might be suitable for the purpose he envisaged. From the roof beams he could see that it was structurally in good shape. He was beginning to understand the construction of buildings as well as he understood the construction of furniture, and his belief that he could take on the enormous task of converting a rambling and neglected historic house reflected his growing confidence in his abilities as an impressario of architecture.

Five times the Parnham property had been sold subject to contract. Five times the sale had fallen through. The Rolling Stones had considered it as the site for a sound studio; the Liberal Party had wanted it as a headquarters to serve their strong political base in the south-west of

England; privileged private purchasers had sought to buy it; developers had wanted to turn it into luxury apartments. But Parnham House was considered too daunting a challenge for anyone to take on. Except John Makepeace. It took a real visionary to look beyond the immediate problems and recognize its potential, and Makepeace was not one to be deflected by doubt. Later, when asked how he had summoned the courage to begin the marathon restoration of Parnham House, he replied: 'There was no question of courage. It was just so obviously and compellingly the right thing to do. If a vision is strong enough, then it becomes self-fulfilling.'

Below: *Parnham House in the eighteenth century, when it was the country seat of Sir William Oglander.*

Right: *Nineteenth-century additions to Parnham House by the Regency architect John Nash reflected the popular vogue of the period for Italianate castellations and pinnacles.*

There were no sales brochures about the house for Makepeace to peruse. He had made the trip down to Parnham on the basis of a photocopied list of rooms and an illustration in *Country Life* magazine. He had come with few expectations but the potential of Parnham filled him with excitement. What he needed to know, however, was whether he would get permission for the change of use required in order to convert the former stables into workshops and to turn the west wing into student quarters. On his second day at Parnham he decided to press the issue. He held a meeting on the site with the local planning officer, fire officer and building inspector. All three knew Parnham House inside out. They advised on the zoning of the building for different purposes and reassured him that they would not stand in his way. Thus Makepeace's move to Parnham was given tacit approval almost immediately.

Parnham House, the Seat of Sir Wm Oglander Bar.^t

There were strong reasons for supporting the establishment of a furniture-making community at Parnham. The Dorset manor house, a listed building without an occupant, was in a state of decay and the local authority was faced with the bill for maintenance. Makepeace's activities would not only give the site an independent future but in time would also provide a welcome addition to the local economy. It was not surprising, therefore, that the Member of Parliament for the area added his voice to those urging Makepeace to move in.

The Parnham estate had at one time comprised 22,000 acres (8906 ha) throughout the West Country, but over the years this land had been gradually sold off. For sale was the house itself, occupying 28,000 square feet (2604 sq. m), and fourteen acres (5.6 ha) of garden. That brought the seemingly impossible dream of a country seat within Makepeace's reach. A price of £96,000 was agreed. To buy Parnham Makepeace was forced to sell everything he owned,

not just Farnborough Barn but also a portfolio of properties in the Midlands which he had acquired and restored as a second string to his furniture-making bow. He succeeded in divesting himself of all these despite the fact that the property market was in the depths of a slump and that Farnborough Barn itself was threatened by a motorway extension: no mean achievement.

Makepeace's commitment to the new Dorset setting was total. 'The listed status of the building meant that it had not been tampered with structurally', he says. 'I was confident in my own judgement of its architectural suitability. The logic of the deal became irresistible.' It was not, of course, only logic that persuaded him. The immense architectural quality and stunning beauty of the house made ownership a thrilling prospect. Much of Parnham's romantic and colourful history is reflected in the building itself, and it was essential for Makepeace to understand the process of its historical evolution if it was to retain its original character.

Parnham literally means 'valley of pear trees'. The present building was constructed in 1540 on the foundations of a house dating from around 1400. The Great Hall initially had a central fireplace and no floors above, and it was divided from a pantry and buttery by a screens passage. By 1585, however, this medieval building was already being remodelled to reflect the new ideas of symmetry emerging in Renaissance architecture: north and south wings and east and west porches were added so that Parnham conformed to the 'E' plan favoured by the Elizabethans.

In 1810 the house was enlarged and remodelled in the Gothic style by the fashionable Regency architect John Nash, who added pinnacles and battlements to the outer walls and built a dining room behind the Great Hall. If Nash's contribution to Parnham was to embellish the fabric of the building, that of Vincent Robinson, an eccentric antiquarian and friend of Sir Henry Cole (founder of what was to become the Victoria & Albert Museum, London), was to ornament the interior. He bought the property and adjoining farms in 1896 for £6,500. Robinson was an avid collector of Renaissance furniture as well as porcelain, rugs, armour and glass. So Parnham became a showcase for fine artefacts from all over Europe fully eighty years before John Makepeace opened his studio there.

Robinson's interiors at Parnham were almost unbelievably rich and ornate. He produced a limited-edition book whose plates illustrated pieces from his collection of applied art. After his death it proved impractical to transport his entire collection to London for auction so Parnham's new owner, the Belgian-born entrepreneur Dr Hans Sauer, who had bought the house and all its contents in 1910, held a five-day auction on the spot. It realized £22,000 and the money was used to renovate the property.

Sauer, who had made his fortune out of mining in South Africa, restored the Tudor features to the Great Hall and other rooms at Parnham. During the renovations a small music room, hidden for a hundred years, was unblocked. Sauer understood about excavations and earthworks, and set to work landscaping the gardens. He built terraces, gazebos, balustrading and a front court, spending a fortune very

Left: The Painted Staircase at Parnham House, complete with ornate Italian alabaster urn, grotesque masks that punctuate the frieze, and large trompe l'oeil murals painted by Royal Academician Talbot Hughes in the 1930s.

Below: A Flemish seventeenth-century stained glass window in the Oak Room, depicting the religious theme of St George and the Dragon.

quickly. These improvements were largely inspired by the chateaux of France, and some were considered by locals, critical of his approach, to be too stark, but all his work was carried out to the highest standard. Sauer moved on from Parnham to Ireland in 1913. His son was to become a professor at Sydney University, and years later, during a lecture tour of Australia, Makepeace was approached by two students who announced themselves as Sauer's granddaughters. 'You live in the house that ruined our grandfather', they told him.

During the Second World War Parnham was requisitioned for military use. It became first a military hospital, then a base for the 16th Infantry Division of the United States Army. A well-guarded room, which is now John Makepeace's drawing office, was used for planning the landings at Omaha Beach in Normandy, which helped to liberate Europe from the Nazis. Parnham was sold in the mid-1950s, minus the home farm and adjacent woodlands, to MIND. Could this dark, damp, smelly place recapture the architectural glories it had acquired under John Nash or the landscaping ideals of Hans Sauer? Could the house again be a lively focus of the applied arts, as in the days of Vincent Robinson? There was no shortage of historical precedents for John Makepeace to follow as he began work on the renaissance of Parnham.

The Great Hall at Parnham House as it was in Victorian times (below) and how it looks today (right) – a dynamic setting for contemporary art and craft.

Right: *The Phoenix Chair, designed by John Makepeace in bleached oak, burr elm and holly, and photographed against the ancient panels and stonework of Parnham House. The theme of the chair – the capacity for natural renewal, symbolized by the rising young shoots of holly that form the back – could apply equally to the house itself.*

Below: *Map showing the layout of the various elements of Parnham that are open to the public.*

Overleaf: *An aerial view of Parnham reveals the scale of the restoration work to house and garden which needed to be undertaken.*

Once planning permission for a change of use had been obtained from the Department of the Environment, the refurbishment programme could swing into action. At weekends during the summer of 1976 Makepeace and his brother moved 200 tons of timber from Farnborough Barn to Parnham. In August, the furniture studio, machinery and work-in-progress followed, with the loss of only two working days. The workshop staff took up residence in the west wing until they found new homes in the area.

The early months at Parnham were 'like camping', recalls Makepeace. 'The place was astonishingly unloved. It stank. There were cockroaches. Yet we were all excited by the venture and believed totally in what we were doing.' His first wife Ann worked hard to make the place habitable and provided endless meals for the staff and the band of workers on the site. Makepeace had set himself a demanding schedule for restoration. The following spring the house and gardens at Parnham were to be opened to the public and, by the summer, the residential school was to accept its first intake of students. Both objectives were successfully met.

The plan for the renovation of the building was to treat the rooms as independent entities in order to bring out their individual characters. In that way, the house could be opened to the public gradually, room by room, as funds permitted. 'We wanted to enhance the diversity of the house, not impose a single aesthetic', explained Makepeace.

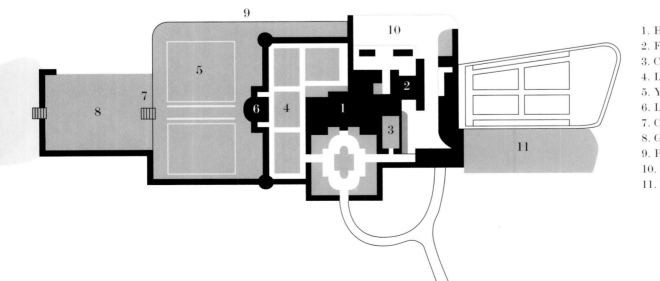

1. House
2. Furniture Workshop
3. Courtyard Garden
4. Ladies' Terrace
5. Yew Tree Terrace
6. Lion's Head Fountain
7. Cascades
8. Great Lawn
9. Picnic Areas
10. Car Park
11. Italian Garden

In 1977 the Great Hall and the Oak Room were restored and opened to the public. The Great Hall was built by Sir Robert Strode in 1554 and remodelled by John Nash, who repositioned the fireplace, in the early nineteenth century. Today the hall not only continues its original function as the ceremonial heart of the house but has also become the main display area for the Makepeace Studio furniture. The Oak Room was built in the early seventeenth century as a kitchen and buttery and extensively restored by Hans Sauer, who lowered the floor, added a fine plaster frieze and Flemish stained-glass windows; it now functions as a restaurant on open days.

Left: *Dynamic topiary on the south terracing of Parnham House forms the view from the Strode Bedroom and reflects the influence of abstract modern art as well as Jennie Makepeace's determination to make the gardens at Parnham a memorable experience.*

Below: *The Strode Bedroom, with its giant yew bed (originally made in John Makepeace's Banbury studio but never sold) and new decorative frieze painted by Jennie Makepeace in 1994.*

Below: *The Strode Bathroom, lined with vitreous tiles from the 1920s and eclectically furnished with an adjustable dentist's chair from the same period, its anthropomorphic profile demonstrating John Makepeace's belief that even the most highly engineered objects can take an organic form when related to the human body.*

Overleaf: *The Drawing Room, with its classical architraves and bleached and lime-waxed panelling, was chosen as a gallery to exhibit the work of contemporary artists.*

A new and important character, Jennie Moores, had by now entered the Parnham story. John Makepeace had been introduced socially to Jennie by an apprentice in the workshop not long after he had arrived at Parnham. She had lived locally since moving to Dorset from the Midlands at the age of seventeen and was looking for work. Jennie had exactly the right combination of skills needed for the job of restoration: tenacity and strength allied to artistic flair. She was also highly practical: she had assisted her mother in renovating old properties in and around Beaminster and had been farming in the next village for ten years with her

first husband. As a local, Jennie knew Parnham House as 'a fairytale castle hidden in the woods'. She had even dressed in Edwardian costume and entertained at garden parties when Parnham was still a nursing home for the elderly. In 1979, two years after the move to Parnham, Makepeace's first marriage had come to an end; four years later, in 1983, he married Jennie, and she and her two young sons came to live at Parnham. Makepeace and his new wife made a formidable partnership.

Work on the restoration of the Drawing Room was carried out by Jennie in 1978. She stripped all the timber panelling of its dark stain and varnish with double-strength caustic soda, and then bleached and lime-waxed it. A lime-wood carving of fruit and flowers around the fireplace was restored and coloured, and Venetian crystal chandeliers by Vistosi were installed to illuminate a gallery in which to exhibit the work of visiting artists and craftsmen. 'We both love colour', says Jennie. 'Over the years we have become braver and bolder in our approach. I have certainly been very influenced by abstract modern art – and by the many artists and designers who have exhibited in the house.'

The Strode Bedroom, part of the sixteenth-century solar, with south- and east-facing windows, was also restored in 1978 together with its adjoining bathroom. Its centrepiece is a giant bed made in Makepeace's Banbury workshop from a single English yew tree. In 1994 the plaster frieze was painted by Jennie Makepeace. The renovation of other rooms, including the King's Room and the Country Room, followed later. Today, only one room in the main house – the Nash Room – is kept for the private use of the Makepeaces and is out of bounds to visitors.

One of Jennie Makepeace's chief contributions to the restoration has been the design of the gardens at Parnham. 'My work on the gardens has expressed my secret feeling that I'd like to be a painter', she reflects. 'What I've done is use the garden as a canvas, and plants and flowers as a medium for colour.' The gardens had been roughly maintained over the twenty years before Makepeace acquired the property, but nothing had been planted. 'They had beautiful bones – all they needed was some clothing', says Jennie. She started replanning the gardens in 1979, beginning with a walled area running east to west, intersected by flagstoned paths with squares of grass and borders, and gradually worked her way right round the property. 'As we are open to the public twice a week, it was essential to create a garden both pleasing and challenging', she explains. 'I wanted to express a sense of peace and of grandeur. It was important that visitors should see many great trees as well as a number of unusual plants.'

The terracing to the south leads down to a lake – created by Hans Sauer and re-excavated in 1988 – through some wonderfully effective topiary which is expertly managed by the Parnham gardener, Jerry Burgess. Spring-fed rills between the yew trees were restored in 1987 by former engineer Ken Loose. A ha-ha wall separates the lowest terrace from the old parklands. 'It is extraordinary how much two or three people can achieve in fourteen acres', says Jennie Makepeace, who has done all of the planning, and most of the planting, and continues to do much of the aftercare herself. 'At the turn of the century there were nineteen gardening staff and the head gardener rarely removed his top hat and white gloves!'

The herbaceous borders, each with its own individual colour scheme, are really for the benefit of visitors, she says. 'Personally, I'd like the gardens to be more wild and woolly. Foliage is as important to me as flowers. I'd like to let things seed and spread, like meadow gardening, instead of mowing them off. John likes the planting in each area to respond to the architecture and surrounding landscape.' What they share is a love of the unorthodox. They also delight in the unexpected. If you look closely at the heron at the edge of the lake, you realize that it is made of wood. However, it serves a practical purpose: it scares the real birds away and protects the fish. As you wander along the river bank, between the trees you catch sight of two startling figures, a giant blue sculpture of comedians Morecambe and Wise by artist Nick Munro. It is so out of context in the Dorset countryside as to be, well, laughable. It signals that this is no ordinary stately home: it is a world where traditional crafts meet contemporary life in the most unusual and compelling way.

The Morecambe and Wise sculpture originally featured in the *British Genius* exhibition in Battersea Park, London, organized by the architect Theo Crosby, and it was brought to Parnham on permanent loan in 1979. Another sculpture, carved from Portland stone by John Maine, stands at the centre of the new courtyard garden, whose formality is softened by the grey and silver plants around its walls. Makepeace first saw the piece in an exhibition entitled *The Condition of Sculpture* at the Hayward Gallery in 1975 and offered Maine a table in exchange.

A visit to Parnham House today is an aesthetic delight; it is a place where nature and artifice elegantly complement each other. But living there through the early days of restoration was not always so pleasant. 'We had no heating in the house for the first twelve years. It was freezing', recalls Jennie Makepeace. 'No heat was bad for the furniture and bad for the building fabric.' There were also occasional disasters, like the time a water tank burst in the roof space and leaked into the floors below. For the most part, however, the fact that every part of the house was being used meant that potential problems could be identified and addressed at an early stage.

Parnham was originally designed with the intention that the large public rooms would be for the exclusive use of the family, with back-of-house facilities teeming with staff. Today, that plan has been spectacularly reversed by Makepeace without needing to make any significant alterations to the way space is divided: the large rooms are open to the public while the servants' quarters are now the students' quarters, providing seclusion for study. It was the ability to accommodate new patterns of use within the original layout of the building that cleared planning hurdles during the refurbishment programme.

Restoration work in an ancient house as large as Parnham will never be completed; it just goes on and on. One should not underestimate either the pressures of inhabiting a home that is constantly open to the public gaze. 'Like living in a goldfish bowl' is how Jennie Makepeace describes it. Certainly the skilful restoration of the house as a showcase for contemporary furniture has drawn visitors in ever-increasing numbers. Today 18,000 people a year visit Parnham. John and Jennie Makepeace's principal aims in carrying out the massive restoration programme were, however, not only to revive the spirit of the place for the enjoyment of visitors but to create an environment that the students of Parnham would find conducive to creativity. In both they have succeeded superbly.

The School for Craftsmen in Wood was launched at a press reception in April 1977, just nine months after Makepeace had moved to Parnham House. *The Times* was supportive of its objectives, pointing out that 'There exists in this country a fearful chasm of inability – technical, commercial and purely sensible – into which too many art-school trained designers fall.' Others dismissed the school as an elitist venture for the non-academic children of the rich.

Makepeace chose the name of his new educational initiative with care. 'School' suggested to him a mature enterprise, akin to a faculty in a university, as well as the encompassing of a broad philosophy. 'Craftsmen' referred not simply to the exponent of a technical skill but a determination to strive for the highest quality. 'Wood' focused attention on a neglected medium (most three-dimensional design courses were then concentrating on wood, metals and plastics). 'Students were denied an intimate relationship with wood, unlike a goldsmith or potter who gets close to his material', he says. (Fourteen years later, following pressure from students who felt that the school's title failed to reflect the strong design emphasis and the number of women on the course, the name was changed to Parnham College.)

The school was given charitable status under the auspices of the Parnham Trust, which was founded early in 1977. Its members included important figures in Makepeace's career, among them Norman Leyland, the founding director of the Oxford Centre for Management Studies, architect Richard Burton of ABK and Orlando Oldham of the Oldham family of industrialists. Each trustee came from a relevant profession. Today the Parnham Trust is not only responsible for the residential college at Parnham but is also the owner of Hooke Park. From the start it was vital to separate the Makepeace Studio from the School for Craftsmen in Wood. The Parnham Trust could not be responsible for the upkeep of a large listed manor house, so the school became a tenant of Makepeace's company, which had bought Parnham with this in mind.

Makepeace set about developing an educational programme for his new venture and calculating its operating costs. He discussed the project with Peter Gorb of the London Business School, who forecast that the school would be under pressure to double in size within five years. But Makepeace resolved to limit its growth. In all his activities he believes in 'small cells of excellence'. As Parnham approaches its twentieth anniversary, its two-year course still has the same number of students (twenty-two) as when it began. Part of the continuity of the school is due to the administrator, Maggie Brook, and the principal, Robert Ingham, who were there at the start and remain key educational figures at Parnham today. Ingham, an expert maker, had trained as a furniture designer and run a workshop in North Yorkshire with his brother. He had also gained experience as a craft teacher and as an interior design retailer. This combination of skills, spanning design, making, education and sales, fitted the Trust's needs precisely. 'I'd heard of John Makepeace but had never met him', recalls Ingham. 'I saw the job vacancy by chance and it seemed to be the vehicle that I was looking for. I had developed my own teaching rationale and was very much in sympathy with John's vision of a self-sufficient school. At Parnham we were able to develop our programme with an immediacy other institutions were not in a position to match.'

By May 1977 the School for Craftsmen in Wood had selected its first ten students. Fees – set at £3,000 a year to cover the high running costs of such an intensive residential operation – did not deter applications, even though the fees for Eton, Britain's most famous public boarding school and one of the most expensive, were only £2,500 a year at that time. 'Despite the high fees, people with real courage, conviction and energy made the tough decision to be the guinea pigs', says Makepeace.

To convert outbuildings at Parnham into student workshops and residential accommodation was going to cost £100,000. An appeal was launched in January 1977, using a simple two-page document outlining the school's aims. Fund-raising today, as Makepeace ruefully acknowledges, is a much more sophisticated and competitive business than it

Right: *Flight Screen, comprising a series of light loops in cherry and ash, designed and made by Jeremy Choppen, a 1994 Parnham College graduate.*

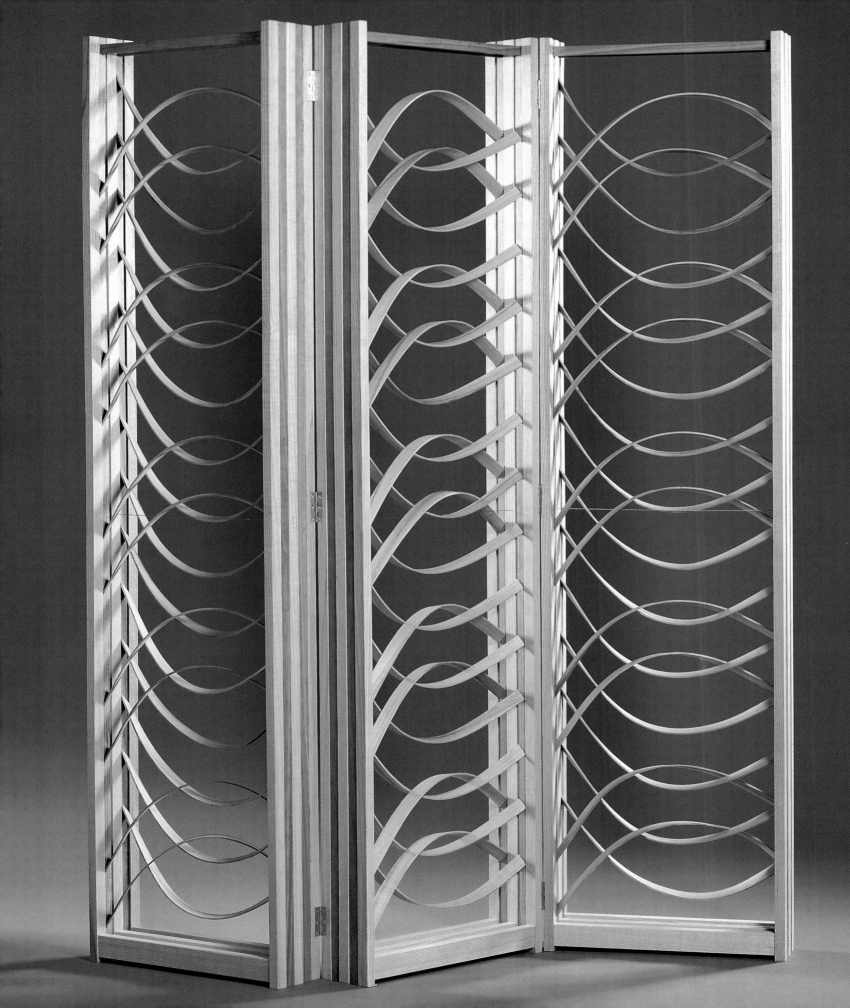

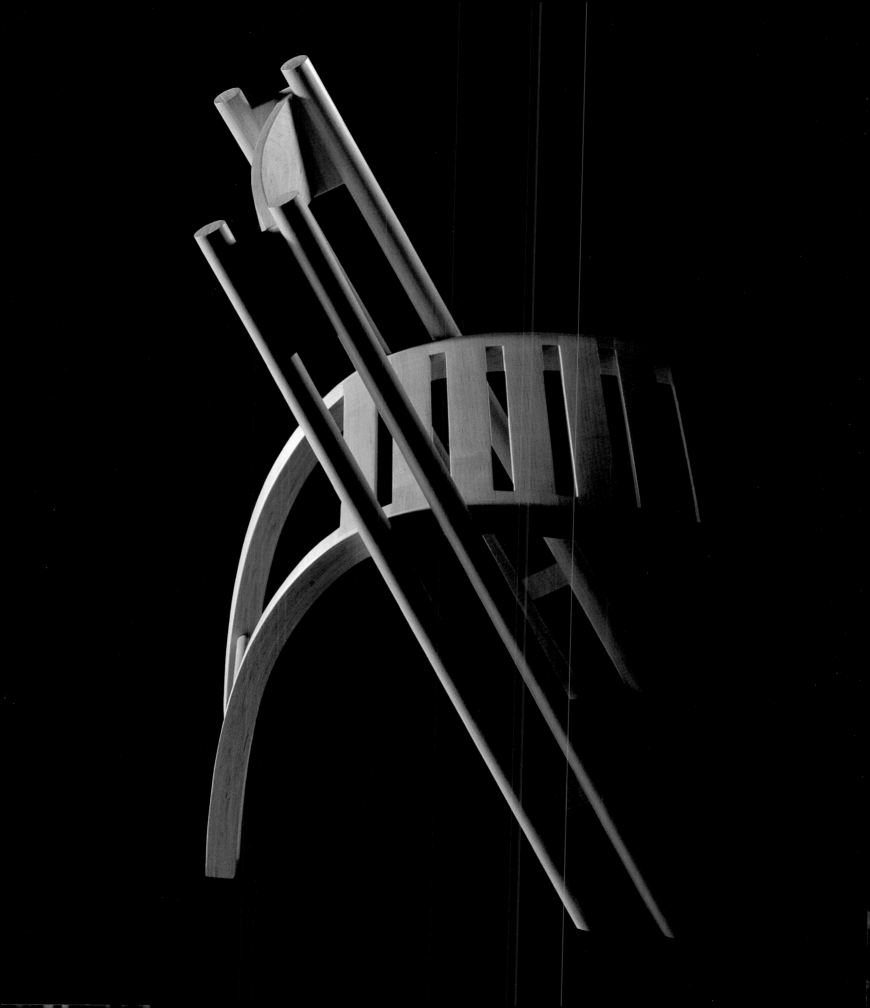

was then. 'I knew nothing about fund-raising. It was done in a crude, instinctive way. There was simply an unstoppable momentum to events', he recalls. In June a £15,000 grant from the Crafts Council was pledged to cover the initial costs of converting the workshops. Contractors were appointed to complete the work by September. Robert Ingham designed and built the kitchens, and Bim Burton, son of architect Richard Burton, assisted in many aspects of the conversion and decoration work before joining the college as a student. Other financial contributions followed, including grants of £30,000 from both the European Community and the Rural Development Commission and a donation of £20,000 from Orlando Oldham; private and charitable trusts contributed the remainder.

In September 1977, in an atmosphere of mounting excitement, Makepeace and Ingham were able to welcome the first students into the school. The opening was accompanied by a fanfare of national publicity. In the course of the first year the Duke of Edinburgh visited Parnham and Sir Roy Strong wrote a feature on it for *Vogue*, which was accompanied by photographs of the house and gardens by The Earl of Snowdon.

In the early days Parnham students were predominantly self-funding British school-leavers aged around eighteen, from affluent backgrounds. The idea of the course clearly caught the imagination of young, privately educated people looking for a purposeful alternative to a career in the City or in industry. One such was The Earl of Snowdon's son, David Linley, whose enthusiasm to learn the skills of furniture making was aroused by a lecture given by Makepeace at Bedales school in 1978. The royal connection helped to give Parnham the cachet of high society, and a training there was seen as an elitist undertaking. However, the public school profile of the student intake has changed a good deal over the years. The first overseas students were admitted in the second year, and gradually the course attracted a significantly higher proportion of mature students from different backgrounds. Many of them were married, with their own families, and without the means to finance themselves through the course. Students are not allowed to start the course unless funds are in place for the full two years, and a network of charitable trusts and bursaries was established to

Left: *Brasserie Chair in maple, designed and made by John Souter, who graduated from Parnham College in 1993 and today runs his own furniture-making workshop in Perthshire, Scotland.*

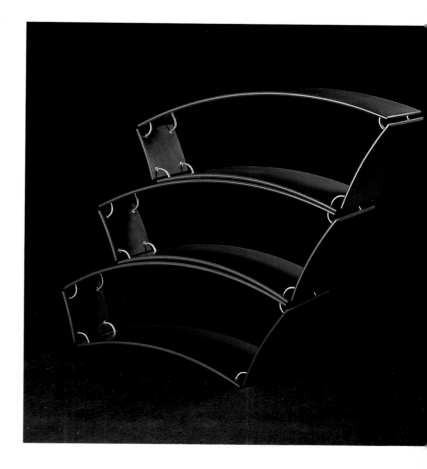

Above: *Lean On Me bookshelves in stained and oiled medium-density fibreboard, designed and made by Florian Harmer, a Parnham College graduate in 1995.*

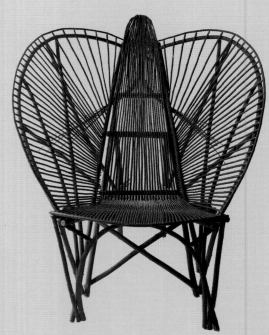

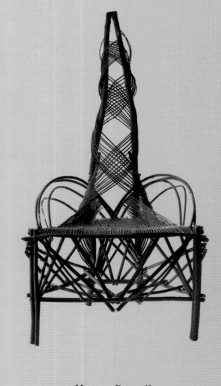

John Morey   *Guy Martin*   *Marcus Boswell*

Keith Lobban   *Oliver Dunn*   *Nick Bentley*   *Jeremy Choppen*

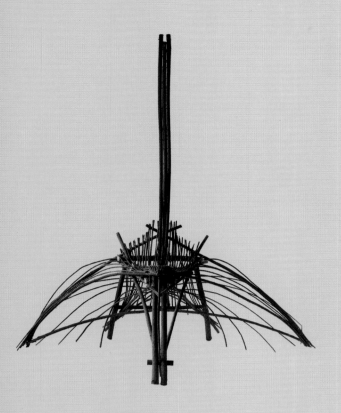

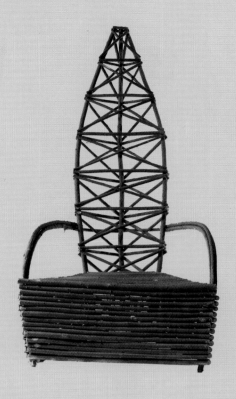

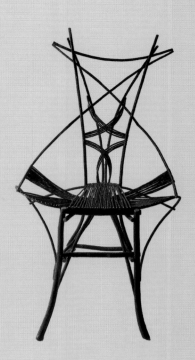

Hans Christian Usadel

Adam Shorrock

John Callen

Esther Hall

The diverse sculptural results of a three-day student project at Parnham College, led by the American craftsman Clifton Monteith with Guy Martin as design tutor. The highly imaginative chairs are made of withies simply nailed together.

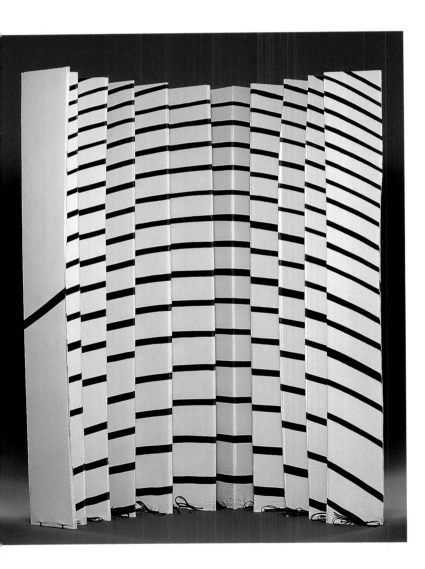

Folding Screen in handprinted calico on plywood, designed and made by Hans Christian Usadel, a Parnham College graduate in 1994. Shoelaces tying the wood slats in place add a witty touch.

support those who lacked the necessary funds. Every year Parnham attracts around thirty serious applications for the eleven residential places on offer.

John Makepeace comments that the applications to Parnham reflect the fault lines in British society:

> 'Many of our mature students are people who were academic high fliers at school and university, and chose highly paid careers in banking, computers or the oil industry but ultimately found their jobs unrewarding. They needed to regain control of their lives and find a new sense of direction, and they have come to Parnham to acquire self-reliance through learning to design and make objects.'

Industrial executives like John Varley – a research manager with the chemical multi-national ICI, who took voluntary redundancy to train at Parnham in the early 1980s – are typical of the trend. Varley explained to *The Financial Times* that he had given up his well-paid job because he had found little opportunity to use his creativity and judgement in a large organization.

One could say that the school at Parnham has been fortunate to have prospered on the back of a broad craft-making revival which gathered momentum in Britain in the early 1970s. But then that revival was due at least in part to Makepeace's own successful example in furniture making over the previous ten years. In the search for an alternative to conventional career paths, the crafts – so neglected a decade before – took on a special cachet among the professional classes. As *The Times Higher Education Supplement* wryly remarked in discussing the new Parnham school: 'Craft work has changed its status. It used to be something to occupy boys who were not up to geography 'O' level but has now become a near cult. Hardly a day passes without cries from the supertax bracket that from now on it is warp and woof for them and the delights of the potter's wheel.'

What greeted students when they arrived at Parnham was not, however, an agreeably relaxed rural retreat but an intense atmosphere in which they were expected to design projects, devise marketing strategies and write business plans as well as learn how to turn wood into furniture. The timetable was deliberately rigorous: an 8 a.m. start in the workshops every day and evening classes three nights a week. The notion that this was to be a soft option for the privileged was swiftly quashed. Ingham recalls the hectic early life of the school:

'It was a day-to-day challenge. The outline programme evolved rapidly into a very full timetable. The initial idea was that I would be the master craftsman with apprentices learning at the bench. In the first year we taught making skills through six major projects. Although we are sited right next to a professional workshop practice, the two operate in parallel but separately. Students get on with their own work and develop their own business ideas. This has always been the case.'

Robert Ingham did most of the teaching in that first year to keep costs down, but very quickly a policy was established at Parnham to bring in as many visiting tutors and lecturers as possible in order to broaden the school's educational base. As Ingham explains, 'Exposure of students to a wide variety of skills, attitudes and experience has always been important. To have only John and me teaching would have been very limiting stylistically.' The business management component of the course was initially run by John Jones. A specialist design tutor – Royal College of Art graduate Mick Bates – was appointed at the end of the initial year to supervise the first cohort in their second year.

The course demanded a certain type of self-directed student, and the Parnham team worked with an industrial psychologist to develop appropriate interviewing techniques. 'We look for people who have a broad range of interests and are likely to succeed in business,' says Makepeace, 'people who are socially well-adjusted, responsive and sensitive to others. We look for judgement in students. What decisions have they made and why? Have they been effective in implementing those decisions? How well do they know themselves? Are they ambitious and realistic?

Designer-maker Rod Wales joined the second student intake at Parnham in 1978. He had trained at Rycotewood College and worked for a spell as a design technician at Buckinghamshire College, a well-known art college in High Wycombe, centre of the traditional wooden furniture industry. Initially he went for a job in Makepeace's workshop but

Case of Chairs stacking display unit in sycamore, designed and made by Brian Reid, a 1995 Parnham College graduate.

was persuaded to apply to the school instead. It was a decision he does not regret:

'The attraction of Parnham for me was being in a secluded country setting with like-minded people. There was a lot of social interaction and the opportunity to meet and work with all these amazing designers and makers who were providing tuition – people like Wendell Castle, Richard La Trobe Bateman and the sculptor David Nash. The teething problems of the course were part of its interest. Everything was new and untried, but it was working.'

During the second year of Rod Wales's course his wife Alison joined Makepeace's professional workshop as a maker. Today Wales & Wales run one of the leading furniture-making studios in the United Kingdom. 'The first time I saw the Makepeace Liberty Table was the first time I'd seen furniture with an art approach', says Rod Wales. 'John was also ahead of his time in teaching entrepreneurship. The three big themes of the Parnham course – making, design and business – created a new approach. You felt you were part of something different.'

The idea of integrating three core disciplines in the course has proved remarkably durable over the years at Parnham. Makepeace acknowledges that the guiding principles that first established the school have remained fundamentally unchanged: 'Every year we raise the issue with the students: how can we change the course? There is always the opportunity totally to rewrite it with a blank sheet of paper. Yet we don't do so.' The reason for this, however, may have more to do with the approach of the principal, Robert Ingham, than with Makepeace himself. Ingham is a classic consolidator and the perfect foil for Makepeace, the restless visionary. 'John feeds on new challenges; he is a catalyst for change', observes Ingham. 'I like a pattern to my life, and a period of time in which the fruits of change can make some long-term contribution. In that sense, I am the anchor.'

Living Table in plywood and maple, designed and made by 1994 Parnham College graduate Esther Hall: a response to a design brief to create an extrovert brasserie chair using low-grade materials and off-the-shelf fittings.

Ash Chair, designed and made in steambent solid ash by Keith Lobban, a 1994 Parnham College graduate. A feature of the Parnham course is that conceptual design skills are counterbalanced by technical and entrepreneurial expertise.

The basis of the curriculum at Parnham is making objects. The course builds on people's innate desire to do things well, explains Makepeace: 'As students gain control over materials and processes they become competent, and confidence flows from competence. Students need to understand why and how things happen. Self-confidence becomes the springboard for exploration and growth as a designer and maker. Making is a fundamental human need and lies right at the heart of the course.'

The first year is therefore largely dedicated to learning workshop techniques. The students are guided through a sequence of processes involved in the making of objects designed by visiting professionals. Many Parnham graduates have commented on the lasting value of this approach, in particular the contribution of Ingham. According to Rod Wales, 'Robert Ingham is uniquely clear and able in,teaching these skills. He demonstrates all the uptight cabinet making techniques without being uptight.' David Linley, who graduated from the college in 1982, pays a similar tribute in his book *Classical Furniture* (1993): 'I was lucky enough to be taught by Robert Ingham, in my opinion one of the best furniture makers in England ... The first lesson at Parnham was a powerful introduction to the demands of craftsmanship.'

The other major strands of the course are phased in gradually in the first year. Visual communication is stimulated by tuition in life, perspective and presentation drawing, and by classes in basic design techniques and the history of design. Similar emphasis is placed on the learning of sound business practice by the business tutor, Andy Christian. Students learn that the high level of practical skill they are rapidly acquiring does not by itself produce objects that are saleable or that will command critical respect. 'Students are encouraged to think about what it takes to turn newly-acquired skills into valued objects', says Makepeace. 'So we begin to explore the idea of design as communication, and the fact that appreciation of objects is affected not only by the content but also by the context of the object.'

David Linley, son of HRH The Princess Margaret, Countess of Snowdon, and The Earl of Snowdon, has emerged as one of the most significant exponents of classical furniture techniques in Britain today. He studied under John Makepeace at Parnham from 1980 to 1982, after hearing Makepeace give a lecture at Bedales school.

On leaving Parnham, Linley began his career from a shared workshop in Dorking where he designed and made furniture. Within three years he had established David Linley Furniture Ltd, now located in Pimlico Road, London, and is an internationally renowned name in the field. In John Makepeace's view, David Linley's success has stemmed from 'his excellence in the presentation of an approach to furniture-making that is coherent and well-considered in relation to his market.'

Linley has not only proved himself as a maker of commissioned pieces, including a giant table for the Metropolitan Museum of Art in New York. He has also become an authority on the subject. He sees his work as being in the tradition of the great classical furniture makers of the eighteenth century, and quotes a play of the period by Oliver Goldsmith as reflecting an eternal principle of design: 'Nothing is truly elegant but what unites use with beauty.'

But Linley has never forgotten the first design principles that he learned at Parnham. As he recalls in his book *Classical Furniture* (1993), 'However eager one might be to show off newly acquired skills, sheer craftsmanship is not enough ... design and craft must work together to create a successful piece.'

Classically styled David Linley hall chair in solid sycamore, with Swiss pear and Varona pear backs and macassar ebony inlaid around the seat rail and down the tapered leg.

The project-based nature of the course could mislead some observers into believing that there is little or no difference between Parnham's approach and the standard Bauhaus-derived curriculum in mainstream British art and design education. After all, most three-dimensional design courses in the United Kingdom seek to build up personal confidence and self-expression through a progressive series of design exercises and projects, interspersed with some cultural and historical studies. But an entirely new element, alien to the moralistic Bauhaus model, makes its presence felt at Parnham: students very rapidly begin to appreciate what their time is worth in monetary terms.

'We are deliberately straight in talking money from the word go', says Makepeace. 'Students quickly learn to evaluate their time, keep time sheets and record the progress of their pieces in order to establish how much they cost to make.' An understanding of perceived value is a more complex issue but emerges from an increasing design and market awareness.

A favourite Parnham ploy is to equate the cost of the course fees with the overheads of running a small business. 'If you know as a student that the fees are costing you £8 an hour, that is very motivating', observes Makepeace. 'At Parnham the students own everything they make, so they take a proprietory interest in the results. Their work is one of their chief assets when they leave the college. Theoretically, they should be able to make pieces during their time here which can later be sold so as to cover the costs of the course.'

The entrepreneurial side of the Parnham course is not popular with all students: the learning of salesmanship techniques, for example, is thought by some to compromise personal integrity. But Makepeace is unrepentant: 'I know that entrepreneurship is usually a dirty word in design. But to me it is a positive one. It is simply about responding to changing circumstances in every sense – social, economic, political, environmental – with ideas and actions. I am an entrepreneur. Entrepreneurship is a creative activity.' He finds the idea that design students should not be exposed to disciplines such as marketing or salesmanship incomprehensible. 'Quality by itself is often not enough. There are no sure paths to success. As a designer-maker, you need to know how

Cabinet of Nine Drawers, fine freestanding furniture by Wales & Wales in natural, ebonized and fumed English oak. Many observers describe their elegant work as belonging not just to the Parnham tradition but to that of Lutyens.

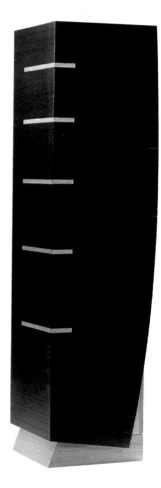

WALES & WALES

Rod and Alison Wales are among the most innovative and respected of John Makepeace's protégés. They represent a new generation of English designers who are interpreting the Parnham school of fine furniture making in fresh and exciting ways. Rod Wales graduated from Parnham in 1980, after studying originally at Rycotewood College, while Alison, a fine art graduate of Reading University, was a trainee in the John Makepeace Furniture Studio from 1979 to 1980.

Together they set up Longbarn Workshop, specializing in high quality one-off furniture and limited batch production furniture and accessories, in a converted farm building in East Sussex in 1981. Since then, Wales & Wales have exhibited in both Britain and Germany, and have developed an international reputation for timeless, intelligent design, often commissioned by architects.

Their public commissions include outdoor seating for the Canary Wharf development in London's Docklands, which reflects the traditions of London's open spaces and parks, and sculptural chess chairs for the Broadgate complex just a few miles away. A ten-drawer cabinet with curved front in English oak has been acquired by the Twentieth-Century Gallery of the Victoria & Albert Museum, London.

John Makepeace says of Wales & Wales: 'What is so admirable about their designs is the timelessness of their approach and their ability to work across a range of materials which is utterly contemporary, always surprising and often delightful.'

Chess Chairs in shotblasted ash and steel, sculptural pieces in a sophisticated architectural game designed and made by Wales & Wales for a central atrium in the Broadgate office development, Liverpool Street, London. The designer-makers were commissioned through architects Skidmore, Owing, Merrill.

Right: *Nicholas Pryke's glass-topped coffee table mixes materials in an enterprising way. The substructure of the table is made of a curved section of solid stack-laminated oak, counterbalanced by three hand-etched panels and held together by brushed stainless steel ironmongery.*

Below: *Corner cabinet in stainless steel with etched glass top by Nicholas Pryke, who graduated from Parnham in 1988.*

to sell the things you make; you need all the disciplines available to you. Learning different disciplines actually stimulates creativity and integrity. Conventional education breaks down our natural abilities into compartments, and in order to function effectively we need to reunite them and learn to use them in conjunction with each other. Makepeace firmly believes that entrepreneurship is a skill which can be learned. 'It is latent in many people and needs to be developed', he says. In the first year of the course professional actors are brought in to coach the students in presenting their ideas more convincingly, an exercise called 'Speaking with Confidence'.

At the end of the first year there is a three-week exchange programme with the Art Institute of Chicago. While American students enjoy a masterclass with Robert Ingham and visit London design practices, Parnham students gain an insight into twentieth-century art, architecture, design and interiors, with visits to the great works of Adler, Sullivan and Frank Lloyd Wright in and around the Windy City. John Makepeace has close links with Chicago, which is the base of the American Friends of Parnham, the foundation which funds the American students.

The Chicago visit is a cleverly conceived part of the Parnham educational experience in that it frames the core concerns of the second year, which has a much stronger design focus. By this stage Parnham students will have mastered a wide range of technical skills and will be ready to extend their repertoire and develop their own design language. The design tutor leads the second year programme. 'It is a year of decision-making and implementation', explains Makepeace. 'Students make commitments to a scheme of work and progress through a sequence of design projects, which gives them experience in defining briefs and working to budgets and deadlines. By doing this repeatedly they learn to organize themselves, to build up their pace and professionalism, and to source their own materials and work effectively in the time available.'

A diverse range of visitors – architects, museum curators, business people – come in from outside to act as 'real-life' clients on key projects. The design tutor is an American designer of furniture and interiors, Alan Deal, who came to Parnham from Detroit in 1994. 'The main design focus is on

Nicholas Pryke came to Parnham in 1986 with a background as an engineer in the construction industry and a portfolio of two-dimensional design work but with no specific woodworking skills. Today he runs his own company, Nicholas Pryke Productions, from a workshop in Oxford, serving both architectural and retail markets with design and making services.

Recent commissions have ranged from contract interiors work, such as a scheme to make reception, shop and café furniture for Nottingham Castle Museum, to product design for retail outlets. Pryke has designed a set of tables for Heal's, and collaborated with Richard Woolf on a range of beds for Liberty's.

Parnham's 'hard-working, claustrophobic atmosphere', he says, taught him the skills he later needed to run a successful business. Indeed, John Makepeace praises Pryke's determination to market himself effectively: 'As a student he was clearly focused, stubborn and a good communicator, whose ability to organize himself and his materials meant that he always came up with distinctive results.'

Pryke's family background gives some insight into his interests. His father is a world-renowned engineering expert on moving buildings, who was consulted on the Leaning Tower of Pisa; his brother is an authority on furniture history. Pryke, however, concentrates on the practical side of his training, and makes constant use of the Parnham network in recruiting makers to produce his designs.

NINA MOELLER

German furniture designer Nina Moeller studied at Parnham from 1987 to 1989, having previously undertaken a craft apprenticeship in Bremen (which included inserting window frames on building sites) and studied briefly with a traditional cabinet maker in France. Parnham, however, opened her eyes to the combination of technical, design and entrepreneurial skills required to survive as a designer-maker. 'The course gives you the courage to go out there and do it for yourself.'

And that is precisely what she has done. Today she runs her own design business from workshops in the Kew Bridge Steam Museum. There, amid some of the most magnificent functioning examples of Victorian engineering in London, she has built up a client base which ranges from private individuals to companies. On larger-scale projects she collaborates with Canadian designer Pat Booth. Together they produced a new stacking chair for The Ivy restaurant in London's Covent Garden.

Dynamic, organic shapes and unusual use of materials mark out Moeller as a confident new talent. 'She achieves quality because she is a good listener and is always able to resist her first thought,' observes John Makepeace. Increasingly, her motivation is towards designing rather than making. 'I have made pieces by hand out of necessity to realize my ideas,' she says, 'but now I am veering more towards design. I want to subcontract more of the making process. I'd rather use my brain than just my hands, although I acknowledge that you need to be able to do it yourself in order to direct others.'

Chaise longue in red beech designed by Nina Moeller, a Parnham graduate in 1989, photographed in the Steam Museum at Kew where Moeller has her workshop.

getting the students to *think*', explains Deal. 'We pull on their reins and ask them to consider how they are going to use all those impressive technical skills they have acquired. The message is that design comes first.' Deal has devised a programme of designing and making which, in the first term of the second year, takes the theme of 'display' (frames, bookshelves, pedestals, plinths and so on) and, in the second term, 'seating', building up in the final term to projects which look at furniture pieces from the triple viewpoints of making, design and marketing. Visual literacy in students is further stimulated by continuing life, perspective and presentation drawing classes, by studying colour theory and 3D analysis studies and by investigations into texture, ergonomics and anatomy.

For Alan Deal, teaching in leafy, rural Parnham offers a marked contrast to the life he is used to in Detroit, one of America's most gritty urban centres. But he is intrigued by the idea of a self-supporting educational community deep in the countryside: 'It is a brilliant concept and a very stimulating environment. The only US college which remotely compares is Cranbrook Academy of Art, near Detroit.' Cranbrook is based at Bloomfield Hills, on a remote rural campus designed in the 1920s by Eliel Saarinen. Its cloistered atmosphere and atelier-style teaching approach is strongly evocative of Parnham.

Since the early 1980s its design graduates, influenced by the powerful philosophical stance of course leaders Michael and Katherine McCoy, have created a particular design movement in America in much the same way that Parnham alumni have done in Europe. But, as Deal points out, Cranbrook has many disciplines – architecture, ceramics and textiles, for example, not just furniture design – and there is less concentration on actually making objects. 'Students at Parnham learn how to take finished products to the market', he says.

This view is supported by Nicholas Pryke, who graduated from Parnham in 1988 and now runs his own design business in Oxford. 'Parnham equips you with the skills to be self-sufficient', explains Pryke. 'Whereas most design graduates have to go out and get a job, Parnham graduates can at least make products which are saleable. This provides some independence from the start.'

As well as an intensified focus on design, in the second year the entrepreneurial strand becomes more pronounced. Andy Christian, who directs the Devon Guild of Craftsmen, has a special insight into the practical problems of running a professional craft business, from cash flow and capital funding to copyright. There is a strong element of competition as the course reaches its climax: students compete for a prize for the best business plan, the Oldham Business Award, and for the Smallpeice Design Award.

THE PARNHAM MOVEMENT

Graduation is marked by high-profile student exhibitions to attract potential clients. In the past, venues have included Sotheby's auction house in Bond Street, London, where students have shown their work alongside pieces by Robert Ingham and the John Makepeace Studio. Parnham graduates have also exhibited at the New Designers summer show at the Business Design Centre in London. Every effort is made to market Parnham's graduates in as professional and presentable a way as possible, resulting in the widespread view that there is an identifiable network of Parnham graduates now active throughout design and craft making in the United Kingdom. 'In the national designer-maker movement, the talents and capabilities of Parnham alumni are well-represented and well-recognized', says Robert Ingham.

Since the course began in 1977 more than 170 students have graduated from Parnham. On completing the course, graduates are not simply given a grade; they receive a full written testimonial. 'There is a lot of personal counselling of students', says Makepeace. 'We help them to clarify their life goals – who they are and what they want to be. The course is structured in such a way as to stimulate the desire to learn an ever-broadening range of skills and achieve deeper understandings. Every student needs a personal guiding vision. I suppose that aspect of the course represents the projection of my own experience and beliefs.'

Former students describe the atmosphere at Parnham as intensely hard-working and often very claustrophobic. 'It was like being in a monastery', says Nina Moeller, a German designer who graduated from Parnham in 1989 and is now running a furniture design business at the Steam Museum at Kew in Greater London. 'You could not run this type of course in a large city. It has its own unique culture. It is very intense and cut off.' Moeller went straight from Parnham to set up her own design and making practice. 'Parnham prepared you in every way, from woodworking to speechmaking', she says. 'We had guest lecturers from all over the world and the course wasn't just about furniture. We would sometimes spend a week making kites or cranes in order to look at structures.'

Alice Robin graduated from Parnham in 1990 and today is manager of Conran Shop Contracts, owned by Sir Terence Conran, in Butler's Wharf, London. 'There was a transparency about the educational process so that you grasped what it was that helped you to learn more', she recalls. 'The core principles of getting things to work as best they could proved transferrable to other fields of endeavour. And the idea that you should invent things, make them, market them and then make a living from them attracted a lot of stubborn individuals to the course. There was an incredible sense of purpose about the place.'

The idea of a Parnham movement, however, makes some of the school's alumni wary. 'There is definitely a Parnham ethos', says Nicholas Pryke, 'but some people are hostile to the idea of Parnham or jealous of it. They also think Parnham graduates will automatically want to design in the same style as John Makepeace, which is not what the course is about.' Pryke, who came to Parnham with no woodworking skills at all, says that the course is sold to prospective students on 'a romantic ticket which is seductive. You then spend the first couple of terms shedding those romantic notions and getting down to the realities of what it takes to make a living in this field. Two camps swiftly emerge: those students, like me, who have design aspirations and those who are simply in love with working in wood as craftsmen.

Munich-based furniture designer Konstantin Grcic, a Parnham graduate in 1987, has realized many of his design aspirations with a range of high-profile commissions from German, Italian and British companies. Today he is one of the most sought-after young designers in Europe. 'Parnham has been the most important fundamental experience in my career', he says. 'Although I have naturally moved on in my work, a lot of the principles learnt during my time there have been very valuable. Parnham is a unique community, an incredible repository of knowledge where you can concentrate on developing your work.'

Makepeace's own furniture-making activities have always created a ready market for the disciples he trains, and the Parnham alumni scattered far and wide naturally compete with their master for commissions – an irony which Makepeace recognized early on. 'As my own workshop grew', he says, 'the nature of my work has changed, so moving to the higher ground and leaving space in the market for students to make less expensive pieces. Obviously, over time, more enterprising graduates caught up with me, producing more ambitious and expensive pieces, but the competition from those trained at Parnham helps to enlarge the market and will continue to do so. I would be concerned if the reverse were true. The ethos of everything we do at Parnham is the pursuit of excellence. The only way the college will attract good students in the future is if its graduates go out into the world and are successful.'

Robert Kilvington joined the Parnham course in 1989 with a background in banking and insurance. It was while working in the Lloyd's Building in London, designed by Sir Richard Rogers, that his interest in design was first kindled. 'I wanted to do something on my own, based upon a natural skill or talent,' explains Kilvington. 'Parnham was therefore very good for me. It was insular and intense, with no distractions. We fitted three years' work into two years by working evenings and weekends. I became completely immersed in it all.'

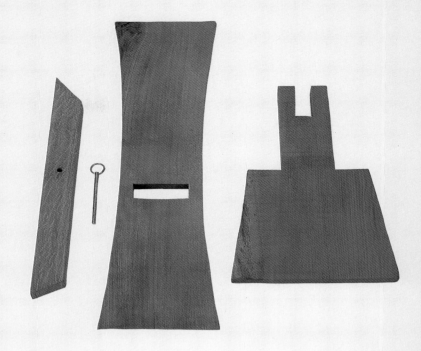

Kilvington found this conscientious craft grounding invaluable when he subsequently studied at the Royal College of Art, London to extend his design skills. Today he runs his own design practice in a studio near Newbury, Berkshire. Recent commissions have ranged from a series of display cabinets for Southampton City Art Gallery to a series of coffee tables for the Italian manufacturer Capellini. Made of Douglas fir with Japanese dovetailed joints, these tables were launched at the 1995 Milan Furniture Fair. However, Kilvington also continues to make and sell a small, sculptural flatpack chair in oak, which he originally developed at Parnham. 'Robert's design talent first emerged during the Parnham programme,' recalls John Makepeace. 'He was sensitive and innovative in the way he used technology to create fresh solutions.'

Flatpack chair in oak with stainless steel pin, designed and made by Robert Kilvington while a Parnham student.

John Makepeace arrived at his creative focus on the integrity and value of furniture as art via a circuitous route. His journey had taken in both the series production of retail artefacts and the collaboration with architects on contract interiors. Far from diluting his vision, these experiences helped to reaffirm in his own mind the reasons why unique furniture pieces should continue to be produced, and what artistic statements they should make about the craft process – and about the people who commission them.

The Times critic Prudence Glynn once wrote that John Makepeace feels about wood as jewellers feel about gold. It was clear from an early age that Makepeace's imagination was totally captured by the properties of the material. As he says, 'No two pieces of wood are ever exactly the same. That's a mind-bending thought.' One can see in his workshop the use of techniques to exploit the visual and structural qualities of wood in the most spontaneous ways possible.

In the pursuit of quality Makepeace had decided early in his career to train his own workshop staff. He found that craftsmen from the furniture industry were generally not equal to the standards he required and that he achieved better results by training school-leavers. David Pearson, for example, joined the workshop at Farnborough Barn in 1968 as a woodworking apprentice. Today he is responsible for timber seasoning and selection and for all machine operations in the Makepeace Studio workshop. There was also an increasing demand from Royal College of Art graduates for the opportunity to work at Farnborough Barn in order to gain practical woodworking skills and experience in preparation for launching their own businesses. David Field and Ashley Cartwright were among Makepeace's early protégés who have since gone on to establish their own reputations in furniture design.

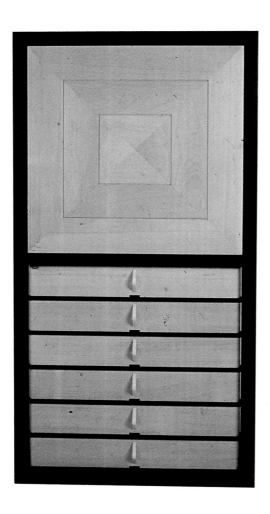

The more successfully Makepeace trained his craftsmen and the more confident he felt about their ability to execute his designs, the more he began to question his own time-consuming role as a maker. By the early 1970s his life had become infinitely more complicated, involving consultancy tours and travel as well as the subsequent challenge presented by the acquisition of Parnham. As a result, he was forced to work on new pieces late into the night, which was exhausting. His only option was to relinquish the task of making and confine himself exclusively to his design and advisory roles in the workshop, a decision that anticipated the transition to Parnham. He needed to be free to concentrate on organizing the move, a large-scale logistical exercise in itself, on fund-raising for his new educational venture and on setting up the Makepeace Furniture Studio workshop. The last piece he made by hand himself was a stunning geometric double-sided desk in South American macassar ebony, holly and buffalo suede, with cedar drawer linings and ivory handles. Appropriately enough, it was featured in *Design* magazine.

Once the workshop was up and running at Parnham, Makepeace evolved new ways of working with his craftsmen at the bench so that as a designer he could be part of the exploratory creative process of making without actually needing to put in all the hours required to produce the perfect dovetail. Nearly twenty years later, his own background as a furniture maker informs his daily dialogue with his craftsmen and invests his artistic direction with a special resonance, as those closest to him in the workshop fully acknowledge.

Left and right: *The last piece that John Makepeace made by hand in the mid-1970s. It is a geometric double-sided desk of macassar ebony, holly and buffalo suede, with each component carefully constructed and finished.*

Previous page: *A maquette of the two-seater Embrace Bench sits on the finished product, revealing the process from initial proposal in model form to completion of the client commission. Maquettes not only convey information to the maker, but capture the spirit of the object.*

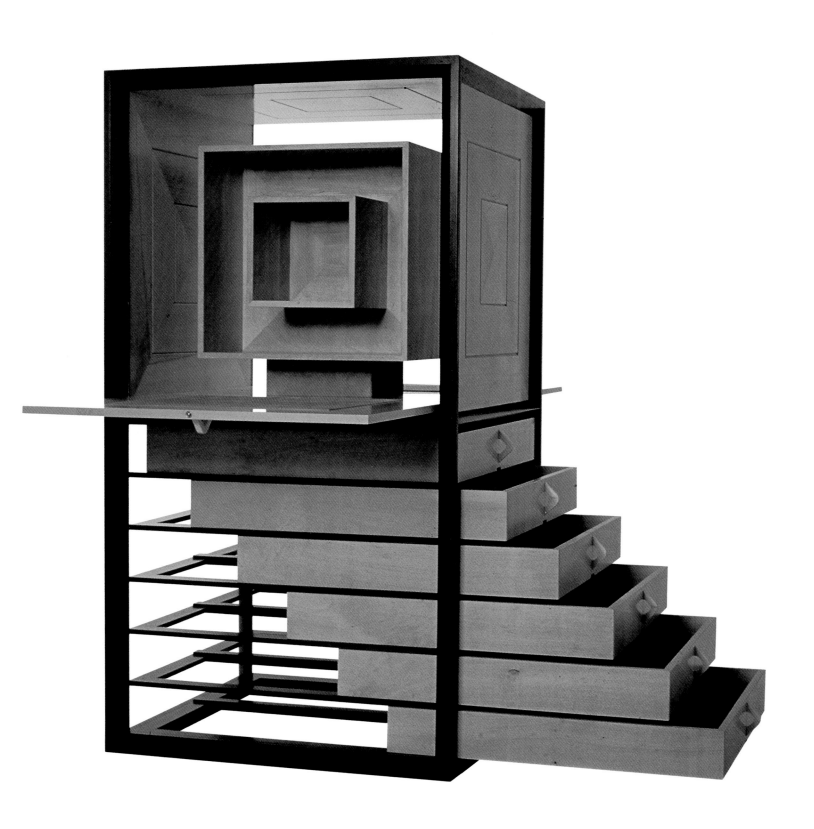

Today the John Makepeace Furniture Studio at Parnham is one of the most widely renowned design workshops of its kind in the world. His team of eight assistants includes Andy Tye, Tom Kealy, David Pearson, Paul Crudge and four apprentices, all of whom play key roles under Makepeace's personal direction.

Each piece is assigned to a single craftsman to make. The day in the workshop starts with a briefing session with individual craftsmen to discuss current projects and monitor progress. Working in this way, Makepeace endeavours to control each furniture commission at every stage of its development, thus extending the design process right through the act of making, continually reviewing designs, materials, processes and details in the search for better resolution in the finished object. Makepeace describes the creation of each piece of furniture as 'a voyage of discovery'. He says, 'An inherent part of the artistry of our work is the continuous interpretation of the design through the making process. As an object is made, so there is a build-up of information in terms of strength, weight, balance and image. This will influence and alter decisions as we progress.' Likening himself to 'a composer who is also a conductor leading an ensemble of virtuoso craft performers', he says 'Not only do I compose the work, I also interpret it through the making process.'

Conventional industrial furniture making regards design and specification as separate entities from the making process, which in itself becomes a routine, pre-legislated exercise. In Makepeace's workshop, however, making is seamlessly integrated into a fluid and highly sensitive design progression. This starts with a series of dialogues with the customer and his design assistant before the craftsman's involvement, and will most likely end with a polished piece sitting in a private house or in one of the most prestigious public galleries in the world.

Left: Senior craftsmen at work inside the John Makepeace Furniture Studio at Parnham House. Each making process is described as a 'voyage of discovery'.

Below: Folding chair in bleached cherry and coach hide. It has a self-locking scissor action when folding which makes it more elegant than a conventional director's chair.

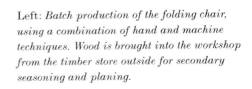

Left: *Batch production of the folding chair, using a combination of hand and machine techniques. Wood is brought into the workshop from the timber store outside for secondary seasoning and planing.*

Right: *The finished object, the result of a dedication to quality in making.*

A display cabinet, designed to protect a model of the HMS Alfred, comprises an elliptical glazed unit with a patinated copper canopy on an open leg structure of curved yew, each element of which traces a line through the three-dimensional volume of space beneath the cabinet. 'Conventional façade-style drawing techniques would struggle to capture the intent of the design,' says Makepeace.

Makepeace has been hailed by some commentators as the Chippendale or Sheraton of the late twentieth century. But however flattering the description, it is quite inappropriate in one sense because he has decisively rejected classical eighteenth-century design methods, which presented both buildings and furniture in façades or elevations. 'While it is appropriate to rectilinear forms, that convention creates objects which lack visual depth', he explains. 'I never design objects elevationally. My work is a response to human form and use; it is about structure, about a fourth dimension working *within* a volume rather than on its surface.' Makepeace believes that much of the predictability of modern furniture derives from conventional design methods which revolve around the drawn elevation and plan. It may make pieces easier to manufacture but it results in a loss of aesthetic wholeness; effectively, it means that the design process dictates the form of the furniture. For that reason, he uses models, maquettes and perspective drawings to convey information to his makers.

In a piece like the Millennium Chair, for example, one can see that a drawing would not have been able to describe the extraordinary trajectory through space of each of the individually shaped elements which make up the curvature of the back. Makepeace has manipulated the materials in such a way that they form a three-dimensional grid which simply cannot be captured on paper. Another project, a display cabinet built for a private client to house a museum-quality model of *HMS Alfred*, demonstrates the same point: the three-dimensional volume of this elliptical glazed unit, which stands on an open framework of curved yew wood, could not have been clearly conveyed in two dimensions. 'Not only is the model more useful to the craftsman in terms of the information it conveys,' says Makepeace, 'it also carries more of the *spirit* of the object.' Some pieces, such as a cabinet for example, may require elevations and plans to convey technical information, but those which are more free-form and open in conception, with elements tracing lines through space, require a different form of communication, he maintains.

In the early stages of his career Makepeace had made extensive use of non-sustainable tropical hardwoods in his work. But in recent years this ardent environmentalist has

Right: *Graduation Cabinet, made of burr olive ash with hickory drawer sides, a maple frame, holly handles and burr elm feet.*

Below: *Making the Graduation Cabinet. John Makepeace's design assistant uses drawings and models to visualize the concept (top left) before the project goes into the workshop. Then the precision process of making begins: drawers are constructed, handles are turned, tambours are fitted. Finally, the drawers are slid carefully into position.*

avoided such materials. The focus in the workshop is now predominantly on English hardwoods – oak, holly, yew, mulberry, ash, cherry and sycamore – and especially on the rarer forms, ripples and burrs, in which some of them are available. The use of rare materials, albeit indigenous ones, puts many craftsmen on the defensive. Makepeace, however, has a simple justification which he illustrates by drawing two pyramids side by side. The pyramid on the left has industrial users of wood in the broad base at the bottom and craft users, such as himself, in the narrow point at the top. The pyramid on the right has pine and spruce, available in

*Detail from the Graduation Cabinet showing
the relationship between frame and drawers.*

abundance, at the bottom and other woods, stacked in layers according to rarity and quality, towards the top, the apex being occupied by such woods as holly and yew.

Makepeace's point is that he does not touch the common materials, at the bottom of the pyramid of resources: these are utilized by the manufacturing industry. He uses only the more unusual woods, towards the top of the pyramid, which have special qualities but are found in such small quantities that industry has no use for them. He therefore sees himself as displaying and celebrating those materials which serve no purpose to manufacturers and would otherwise be wasted.

As a maker, Makepeace has a special fondness for the lightness, colour and sensuous texture of yew, but recognizes the problems associated with it: 'The grain is the most unpredictable of all the English woods and its hot, orangey shade is difficult to use in contemporary interiors.' He also admires the closeness of holly's grain: 'Its almost ivory-like texture makes it exciting to use in contrast with other woods.' Makepeace enjoys combining different materials and has worked successfully on a number of occasions with engineers, blacksmiths, stained-glass artists and textile makers. In fact the Studio output is not confined to woodwork alone and he is constantly on the look-out for potential collaborators in related fields: one object in Makepeace's 1994 Creation Collection, consisting of pieces inspired by nature, is a circular table called Dancing Circle, its slate top resting on a bronze base cast by a sculpture foundry.

For a craftsman identified as a figurehead of an anti-industrialist movement, Makepeace is curiously interested in the precision engineering associated with castings, and even with adapting advances in aircraft technology to the service of handmade furniture. Indeed, a study of his design influences suggests a far stronger technological bias than might have been expected.

Dancing Circle Table, in cast bronze with a slate top, a rare Makepeace departure from working in wood. It shows, however, his Studio's willingness to collaborate with artists and technicians working in other media.

Makepeace equates designing with being a good storyteller. 'To be able to communicate with an audience is an achievement. Designing in wood demonstrates the human capacity to change things. If you discover that at an early age, as I did, it gives you a sense of self-respect and provides an activity to grow through.'

He claims not to be consciously influenced by other designers but to be excited and inspired by their example. It is an important distinction and one which explains how he can cite such a broad array of talented personalities, all of whom have had an impact on his development in some way. They range from art-historical figures to leading exponents of the Modern Movement, from furniture makers to bridge builders and architects.

Left: *Ornate desk by the eighteenth-century French cabinet maker Jean-Henri Riesener, commissioned by Louis XVI and today in the Wallace Collection, London.*

Makepeace has taken from Riesener's work a sense of the luxurious combination of materials and the integral use of cast bronze in flowing three-dimensional forms, rather than as applied decoration. Makepeace's Whale Table (below) which has a top of oysters of mulberry, a gilded underbelly and legs of polished bronze, directly reveals these influences.

The eighteenth-century French cabinet makers Jean-Henri Riesener and Jean-François Oeben, who worked at the time of Chippendale, employed a fabulously intricate orchestration of skills and materials to make a single piece. One elaborately detailed desk might have taken fifteen years to build, involving bronze castings and ormolu decoration as well as the use of marquetry, tambour and many other innovative techniques.

The English furniture maker Thomas Hope, working in the early 1800s, impressed Makepeace with the sheer ebullience and robustness of his pieces. At the end of the nineteenth century the Belgian Art Nouveau furniture designer Henry van de Velde demonstrated the three-dimensional freedom with which pieces could curve through space. Van de Velde's comment that 'a line is a force like all elemental forces – it takes force from the energy of the person who has drawn it' is a sentiment with which Makepeace identifies, just as he admires the Art Nouveau architecture in Brussels of Victor Horta, who expressed similar beliefs in his work.

The industrialized twentieth century has been a time of growing paradox for the craftsman. The Dutch Constructivist designer Gerrit Thomas Rietveld, and the De Stijl Movement of which he was a member, influenced Makepeace's early series production pieces, such as the knock-down table, in the 1960s. The early, inventive work of British architect and designer Eileen Gray, who worked for some of the great French patrons of the Twenties and Thirties, meanwhile demonstrated great ingenuity in its simple clarity and bold, distilled forms. But Makepeace has also absorbed the more elaborate message of Jacques-Emile Ruhlmann, a furniture maker who worked in Paris and Italy in the early years of this century on colourful pieces of ebony and chrome.

Makepeace's attitudes to Modernism reveal a great deal about his art. He cites the American industrial designer Charles Eames as a key inspirational source. Eames was ahead of his time in using techniques from the aircraft industry to create very individual and expressive furniture.

Left: *Makepeace translates this spirit of sensitive technology into Erudition, a study chair in yew, elm and leather.*

Far left and above: *The work of American industrial designer Charles Eames, whose ground-breaking furniture from the late 1940s and early 1950s showed Makepeace that a scientific approach to function and ergonomics need not be sterile, and could indeed be highly individual and responsive to human needs.*

Below: *Scrubbed oak and polished aluminium castings make an agreeable contrast in this pale kitchen table and chairs, entitled Rhythm and commissioned for a private London home.*

Right: *His use of aluminium castings enabled Makepeace to create slim, elegant profiles for wooden furniture while providing strength at joints and junctions.*

Right: *Sir Norman Foster's telecommunications tower in Barcelona, a landmark in the Catalan capital and a symbol of the architect's visionary quality which keeps the dynamic of Modernism alive.*

Makepeace cites a diverse range of design expression in both process and material which has inspired him, from the hard, wooden geometric invention of the Dutch Constructivist Gerrit Thomas Rietveld (below left) to the soft, humanist forms in plastics and leather of Joe Columbo, the radical Italian designer of the 1960s (below right).

As Makepeace comments, 'Eames showed a breadth of vision and a multi-disciplinary understanding. He worked in collaborative ways and used industrial technology to powerful effect without it becoming inhuman. What could be more responsive to human need than his Aluminium Group seating?' But, the work of Eames aside, Makepeace claims that many of the icons produced by the leaders of Modernism are 'functional' only in the meanest sense. 'Modern objects frequently have an aesthetic which suggests efficient industrial methods of manufacturing although this is in fact achieved only through elaborate techniques; they are inconsistent and compromised in concept. Whereas sculptors have not been trapped by Modernism since they are motivated less by style than by values, for designers the opposite is true, with the result that a dynamic new philosophy has failed to evolve in the field of design. In the wrong hands, Modernism can be very sterile.'

Right: *John Makepeace's Trilogy Desk in cherry and bog oak with bronze detailing, which unconsciously echoes Foster's Barcelona tower (see previous page) in its three-sided form and simple resolution of complexity.*

It is not that Makepeace does not believe in fitness for purpose: he is totally committed to function. He simply does not regard such a commitment as automatically eliminating decoration. 'Function needs a more generous interpretation', he says. 'It has been too narrowly defined. It means more than just use. Enjoyment and pleasure are part of the function of an object too.' For that reason, he does not hold entirely with the Modernist ethos of truth to materials – the use of materials in their most direct, undisguised form – arguing that all materials are conditioned by processes and that processes offer scope for illusion, intrigue and theatre in the design of furniture. He does, however, like to use woods in their most natural state, with decoration not applied but accentuating the inherent grain of the material.

The strongest Modern Movement influence, he believes, has come from abstract sculpture, which has taught contemporary designer-makers to look closely at three-dimensional forms. He enjoys creating the sense of fluidity which the flexibility of timber permits: this perhaps explains his interest in the work of Joe Columbo, the radical Italian designer of the 1960s, whose furniture and lighting in plastics relate extraordinarily well to architecture.

The bigger picture of engineering and architecture draws in a number of other influences on Makepeace's work. Isambard Kingdom Brunel, for example, worked extensively with timber and exploited its structural properties on bridges before he ever moved on to newer materials. And the organic lightweight structures of the German architect Frei Otto – especially the remarkable tent-like design of his Munich Olympic Stadium, built in 1972 – were a profound revelation to Makepeace long before Otto ever worked with him at Hooke Park.

John Makepeace regards Sir Norman Foster as a product of the new culture which resulted in the 1960s and 1970s from Frei Otto's views on the use of materials according to their best properties, and the relationship between structure and nature: 'Foster is the finest of the architects. He is artist, visionary, engineer and entrepreneur – the Brunel of our times. He respects other disciplines and learns from them. His work has depth and power and an amazing degree of resolution.' What makes it so attractive to Makepeace is the clarity with which it resolves complex problems and its

Making and design become a seamless process in the hands of the master craftsman. The Trilogy Desk takes shape under John Makepeace's direction in the Studio workshop at Parnham House. The drawers of the piece pivot from a stainless steel column (see right).

Left and above: *The TGV rail station at Lyons Salatos airport in France, designed by architect-engineer Santiago Calatrava. It is an ambitious high-tech structure which is inspirational to Makepeace in its overt reference to the natural world. The station resembles a delicate steel bird, sheltering its platforms with spreading symmetrical wings. The arched spine at its centre suggests it is about to take flight.*

Right and overleaf: *Mercury Desk, designed for the chief executive of a Chicago insurance company. Just as nature and structure are complementary in the work of the architects Makepeace admires, so he explores the tension of structure using natural materials in his own work. The Mercury Desk conveys the powerful idea of an organization reaching out to different parts of the world. Seven panels of burr walnut radiate from the centre; the veins and legs are bog oak. The innovative structural architecture of the piece combines lightness and solidity - like an aircraft wing. The writing surface slides forward to reveal compartments for accessories.*

technical virtuosity. A high-tech building such as Stansted Airport, which lies low in the landscape and has a series of internal structural 'trees', suggests the fresh connections that can be made between the built structure and the natural environment.

In the hands of Foster or Eames or Otto, Modernism is not sterile at all. It is a dynamic design philosophy which, in its more curvilinear high-tech development, is today once again drawing closer to nature. In the sculptural buildings and bridges of the Spanish architect-engineer Santiago Calatrava, Makepeace sees organic references to nature which suggest that things have gone full circle in the course of a single century. Just as, at the end of the nineteenth century, Victor Horta's Art Nouveau buildings adopted the patterns of nature, at the end of the twentieth century Calatrava's TGV railway station at Lyons Salatos airport in France takes the form of a giant steel bird, whose spreading wings shelter the platforms.

The work of talented engineers, such as Sir Edmund Happold of Buro Happold, whose perception that 'technology makes things possible' and can in some way distil or abstract from natural forms, has been essential to this exciting new phase of modern architecture, Makepeace believes. It is significant that two of the people he describes as having had an impact on his work – Otto and Happold – collaborated with him at Hooke Park. Makepeace regards collaboration with other disciplines as a vital catalyst to creativity.

It is, however, the natural world which influences and shapes the direction of his work above all else. As Prudence Glynn wrote in *The Times*: 'The fact that he never includes harsh angles or edges in his work is because in nature's world there is no such thing.' Makepeace recalls standing in the middle of New York one day in winter: 'I saw someone walking along with a stunning bunch of purple irises, highlighted against this totally grey background. It was quite shocking to think we could be in a place so remote from nature.'

One of a pair of chairs made in English holly (one purchased by the Art Institute of Chicago and the other by the Sydney and Frances Lewis Collection in Richmond, Virginia), the Millennium Chair is effectively a three-dimensional graph of the curvature of the human back.

It is a powerful demonstration of John Makepeace's view that 'the design of a chair can take us into new territory', and reflects his constant striving to create new and exciting structural forms which curve through the volume of a space.

Each component is individually shaped to pick up the lines of lumbar and body support. Each element is built up from eleven different layers, bent and twisted to enable the curvature to flow from one end to the other.

What appears to be the grain of the wood is actually the joint between the layers (holly has little or no grain apparent to the eye).

The structure of the Millennium Chair pushes the conventional boundaries of what can be achieved and is the product of a studio environment dedicated to creating the space and time for experiment – prerequisite conditions for innovation to flourish.

Overleaf: *A detail from the curving back of the Millennium Chair in English holly reveals the ambition and resolution of the project.*

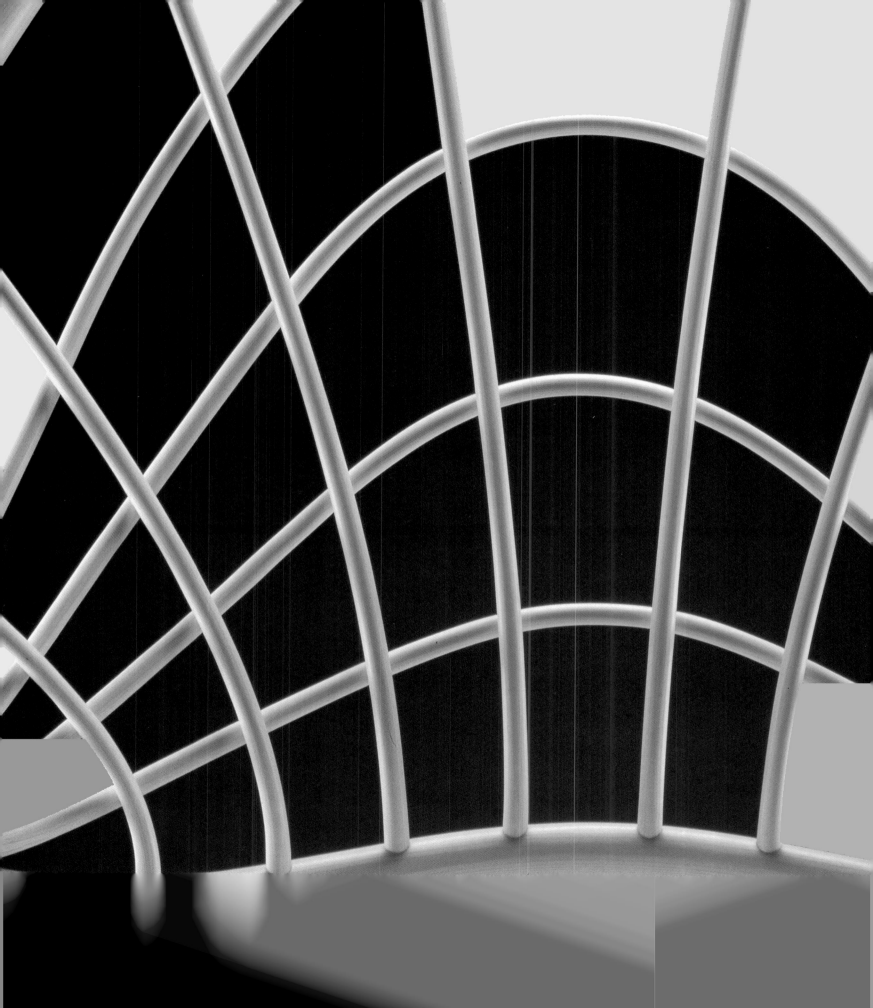

Below: *Making the Standing Stones Table, which features a table top of ancient bog oak strips on a base of scorched 'stones' carved in lime. A senior craftsman reviews progress with Makepeace. Marquetry techniques are used to prepare the strips which give the table top its irregular, striated surface, simulating riven slate.*

Recently Makepeace has begun to employ the patterns, forms and textures of the natural world in increasingly literal ways to make the environmental message of his pieces more accessible to a contemporary audience. His 1994 Creation Collection was conceived as a reaction against the culture of consumerism and as a way to reconnect people with their roots in the environment. One piece from this series, the Standing Stones Table, derives its inspiration from the flat pebble forms on the Chesil Bank, part of Dorset's coastline: a line of carved, scorched stones forms the base, on which sits a riven slate-like top in strips of bog oak. Another piece, Obelisk, a tapering column of drawers in solid yew wood, has a peak which is handcarved to suggest a hilly landscape.

But while there is an abstract quality to Obelisk, other furniture in the Creation Collection uses the most direct and representative interpretations of nature. The carved and coloured foliage of the Vine Chair demonstrates Makepeace's drive to extend his vocabulary of design through the art of making. The Swaledale Throne, carved in lime and either gilded in white gold leaf or dyed black, was inspired by the curly coat of the Yorkshire Swaledale sheep.

Makepeace's Studio has assumed a high profile in the recent revival of woodcarving in Britain, and in 1994 a number of its signature pieces were included in a major Crafts Council exhibition entitled *The Woodcarver's Art*, which toured the United Kingdom. Makepeace recognizes the technical challenge of handcarving and enjoys its fresh, illusionary quality. He is keen that the revival should maintain its momentum. His Ziggurat plinths in the Creation Collection, which were inspired by ethnic pattern-carving and use wood from English oak trees planted at Longleat in 1760, represent perhaps the most strikingly successful examples of this new direction.

Right and overleaf: *The Standing Stones Table was commissioned for a classically restored farmhouse in Oak Park, Chicago. But the inspiration for the piece was much closer to home: the natural pebble forms on the Chesil Bank, part of Dorset's coastline. For Makepeace, the spaces between the stones are as intriguing as the stones themselves.*

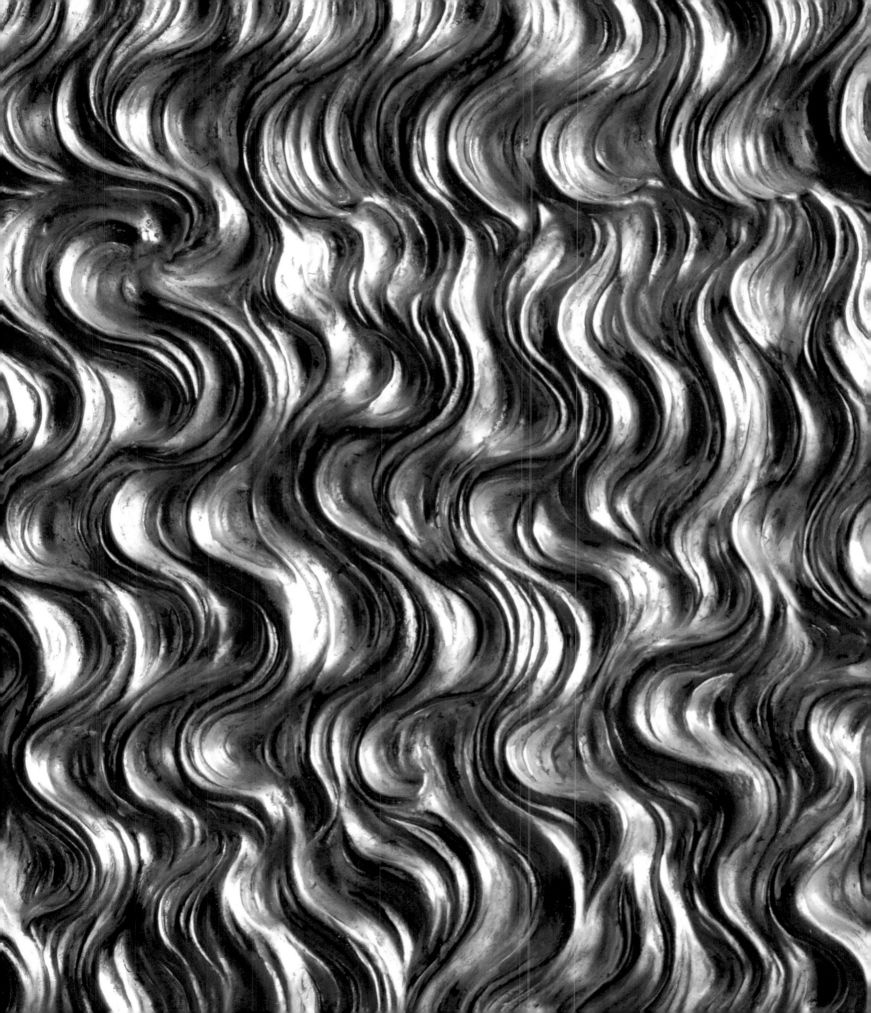

The throne is one of the simplest and most dramatic objects to be found in the entire history of furniture. This throne, carved in lime, was inspired by the fleece of Yorkshire's Swaledale sheep. In black, the rhythmical patterning of the curly Swaledale coat is heightened (left): this is truly the black sheep of John Makepeace's 1994 Creation Collection of pieces inspired by nature.

However, the Swaledale throne has also been gilded in white gold leaf (right) as a visual and tactile expression of luxury, which literally lends a lighter interpretation to the design.

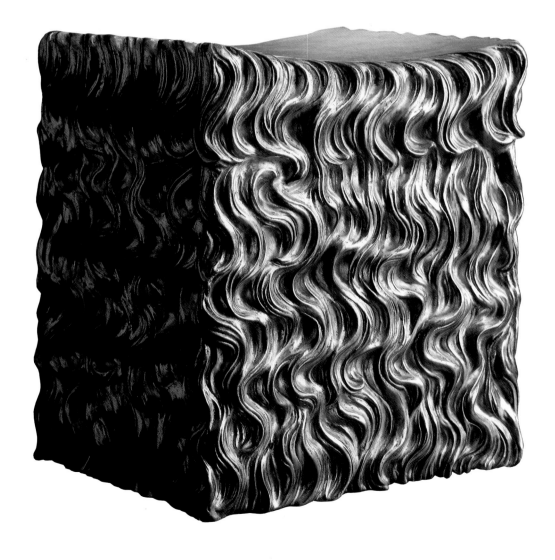

OBELISK

The first obelisks were wooden and predate the earliest stone forms as a monument or landmark. They were cut from tapered trunks of trees and their tops were pointed to shed water. This piece recalls the ancient idea of the monolithic obelisk in a tapering set of drawers in solid yew.

In this single piece so many of Makepeace's artistic preoccupations coincide. There is the luxuriant craft detail in the way the soft undulating sides are shaped to enhance the complex grain of the yew and the drawer handles are delicately fashioned as crevasses within the wood. There is the use of unusual but classically hard-wearing materials: the drawers are made of scented cedar of Lebanon, lined with vellum and running on bearings of hornbeam. There is the abstract interpretation of the environment, in this case an entire hilly landscape crowning the piece (right).

Finally, there is Makepeace's daring use of yew wood, a material for which he has a special fondness on account of its colour and sensuous texture, even though he admits that the grain of yew is 'the most unpredictable of all English woods' and that its hot, orangey colour can be difficult to blend into many interiors.

Obelisk stands out as one of Makepeace's most ambitious pieces in recent years, confirming his role as a risk-taker in design who is prepared to push the boundaries of furniture expression beyond the expectations of his traditional audience.

FEATHER CHAIR

The Feather Chair (right) is carved in lime in a form which
suggests the courting stance of the peacock displaying
the splendour of its tail. Makepeace sought in this piece
to reinterpret a timeless and familiar theme to show how
natural forms can inspire functional objects.

The chair, which was designed as part of the speculative Creation Collection in 1994, provides good support
at the base of the spine and a comfortable soft leather
seat. The most striking aspect of the piece, however, is its
three-dimensional carved decoration, which is revealed as
light moves across its curved form, reminiscent of peacock
feathers caught between sun and shadow.

Below: *Shell Chairs in sycamore and leather,
1990, forerunners in form to the Feather Chair.*

Right: *Front view of the Feather Chair.*

Overleaf: *Rear view of the Feather Chair.*

The Creation Collection is unusual not just in the refreshingly direct way it interprets nature but also because it consists of a range of objects developed by John Makepeace and his team without recourse to a client. Every so often the Makepeace workshop produces a speculative collection such as this, exploring current artistic preoccupations in an unfettered way, but, on average, around two-thirds of the artefacts it creates in the course of a year are made to commission and one-third is made for sale from galleries and from Parnham House.

One could argue, indeed, that Makepeace has been very successful in persuading both individuals and organizations to underwrite his voyage of discovery in furniture. He is on record as warning potential customers not to commission him if they want a safe, predictable object: 'There is little point in somebody coming to me for a piece of furniture unless it produces some fresh dimension which they could not have anticipated.' Of the work which is made to commission, two-thirds is produced for private customers and the balance is acquired by companies, museums and other cultural institutions.

As private customers have come to represent the lion's share of Makepeace's business, he has studied closely their motivations and needs. Both the rich and the famous have commissioned him over the years: fame is not a prerequisite but it certainly helps to be wealthy. His prices are high, reflecting not only the level of craft work that goes into every piece but also the international reputation of the design studio. Yet Makepeace argues that commissioning furniture is neither an elitist nor an esoteric act. 'It is a simple act of faith in the power of art, craft and design to bring joy and meaning to people's lives', he says. 'Patronage of the arts has been a conspicuous element in every civilized society almost since time began.'

His customers come from every walk of life. Makepeace has noticed that self-made people who have been successful in their own career tend to be more confident about commissioning contemporary pieces than those who have inherited wealth. The privileged classes are apt to be conservative in their choice and often already have more furniture than they need. The English preference for antiques rather than new designs is a much discussed cultural phenomenon, which Makepeace has confronted head on by taking an ancient stately home as a showcase for his work. 'You would not even have to make the point in Italy', he remarks. 'Things are beginning to improve in the UK but the patronage of contemporary work has, until recently, been poor.'

A purchase from the Makepeace Furniture Studio is not a decision to be taken on the spur of the moment. Some customers plan and save for up to a decade before finally committing to a commission. The typical profile of a Makepeace customer is a couple in their fifties, enjoying some financial freedom now that their children have left home. Recently, however, new directions in the work of the Studio have attracted financially independent people in their thirties, and the broader ecological values of Parnham and Hooke Park naturally hold an appeal for many young people today.

Another comparatively recent development has been the growth of cultural investment programmes by companies. Makepeace looks ahead to a time when industrial and financial corporations around the world will employ curators to manage their artistic collections, and the purchase of artefacts in the applied arts will be as common as buying paintings or sculpture. A contemporary furniture commission undoubtedly makes a statement to a company's customers, shareholders and employees about the organization itself, and about its values and willingness to sponsor the arts. Makepeace has made furniture for boardrooms throughout his career and has achieved recognition from corporations worldwide. He accepts that committees do not always produce good commissions and that it often takes autocrats of vision to produce the best results.

Two recent commissions reflect the skill of his workshop in making furniture to match corporate aspirations and identity. One is the Mercury Desk, designed for the chief executive of Aon, an international Chicago-based insurance company, to convey the sense of an organization carrying its message to different parts of the world: seven panels of burr walnut radiate from the centre while the legs of the desk and the veins dividing the top are of bog oak. The other is the Forum Group, consisting of tables and chairs commissioned for the new headquarters of Boots in Nottingham. Made in

Right: *The Forum Table and Chairs, commissioned by Boots plc for its new headquarters in Nottingham, reflect Makepeace's belief that furniture making is a branch of the decorative arts on a par with any other. Forum was designed to work in a specific environment in conjunction with the stained glass piece by artist Stephen Newell. The table has a pattern of yew feathers which radiate from spines of bog oak. These spines form the structural ring at the centre and edge of the table. The table legs are braced with polished aluminium castings.*

Below: *A Forum Chair, made of bog oak with polished aluminium castings and leather seat.*

yew and bog oak with polished aluminium castings and leather upholstery on the chairs, they are complemented by striking stained-glass walls by British artist Stephen Newell which light up the interior space around them.

At the start of a private commission Makepeace will explore with his customers the function of a prospective piece and of the room in which it will be placed, any aesthetic and practical aspects to be considered, a provisional programme for the work and an outline of the costs involved. Like a couturier, he is concerned to tailor objects to people's individual needs: 'I am always looking for the particular', he says. 'The analogy would be an architect designing for a particular site.' A new piece may be commissioned for a specific location, perhaps to connect disparate elements in a room. The Prism Table, for example, was commissioned to enhance a narrow hallway in a Belgian house, its decorative floor paved with diagonal patterns of stone and brick. The light strikes the table from adjacent windows and the triangular legs were designed to reflect the light in multiple directions.

Makepeace will visit the space under consideration to sketch and survey it, to understand its proportions and photograph it as a reference to assist the process of design. He will also probe his customers' feelings about other furniture near the allotted space which may have outlived its usefulness, often winning more room for the new piece, thus enabling it to make a more powerful impact.

Private customers tend to be less specific than organizations in defining the purpose of a piece they wish to commission. Makepeace often has to coax out of them the essence of what they wish to achieve. 'It is better to ask them to express it in terms of activities – "write", "display", "store" – what it does, rather than in nouns – "desk", "cabinet", "table" – what it is. Nouns mean different things to different people and can be misleading.' At an early stage he will talk about forms and materials. He carries with him a brochure portfolio of earlier pieces and a box of wonderfully tactile wood samples. Material selection can often spark an interest in a particular approach, acting as a springboard to decisions on the scale and feel of the object. Once there is written acceptance of the brief and budget, design work begins; it proceeds over the following weeks, and the making

process follows approval of the design. This can take from six to twelve months. The customer is part of that process. Having a structure for discussion with customers helps me to get to know them', says Makepeace. 'Very often, through the course of a commission, they become friends.'

Makepeace leads the development of designs in close collaboration with his design assistant. Over the years at Parnham, four successive design assistants have worked with Makepeace, playing a pivotal role in the furniture-making operation. Talking over the brief and the architectural setting, preliminary sketching and brainstorming, will eventually lead to a creative direction. The design assistant will work up the design for daily review with Makepeace and produce coloured perspectives and a maquette if that is necessary to resolve or illustrate the design. These will be shown to the client and discussed and, once everything is agreed, the job will be assigned to a craftsman. Material will be selected by David Pearson and brought into the Studio workshop for secondary seasoning and planing. Makepeace will then work on a daily basis with the craftsman throughout the stages of construction, from the main elements to secondary components such as drawers and pivoting trays, as designing and making become one process. Any sub-contracting that the piece requires – engineering or foundry work, for instance – or the purchase of other materials will be programmed to facilitate a steady progression towards assembly and finishing.

The Makepeace workshop is a demanding, highly organized studio in which craftsmen strive to meet personal targets of excellence which are set at a weekly planning meeting. Only by pursuing the highest standards of professionalism can time and space be created within the work schedule for creative exploration.

The twisting trajectory of a tennis ball in flight is an appropriate metaphor for these seats in oak and leather, designed for an indoor tennis court at an Adler house in Illinois. The architectural setting is significant in shaping Makepeace's approach to client needs.

137

Below and right: *The Prism Table has a top of burr oak and triangular legs of straight-grained oak. It was commissioned for a narrow hallway in a Belgian home, its decorative floor laid with diagonal patterns in stone and brick. Light strikes the piece from adjacent windows. Mindful of the special relationship of table to architecture, Makepeace developed the form of the legs to reflect the light in multiple directions.*

John Makepeace believes that you can place every object in the history of furniture into one of three main categories: the table, the chair and the cabinet. The table relates to architecture in that it is a simple elevation of the floor, a platform which raises the floor to the level at which you need it. The chair relates to people in that it must provide support for the human frame: it is perhaps second only to clothing in its special relationship with the body. The cabinet relates to possessions in that its role is to store and display objects. Each of these categories has its own generic history and vocabulary of form and structure.

Makepeace is a keen student of this vocabulary, and it is possible to trace the progression of his ideas from one piece to another as he explores solutions to the structure and function of an object. What he does not like to do is replicate designs in their entirety: 'Replication tends to result in a loss of quality', he says. 'In making a piece for the first time, all one's efforts are focused on anticipating and solving problems. In a sequel one's attention can be clouded by attempts to recall the way in which the first result was achieved. I believe that can compromise one's thought processes and the clarity of the piece.' He always needs to be moving on. 'We don't accept commissions we don't believe in', he comments. 'Life is too short to be making copies of what already exists.' In this he sounds like the English furniture pioneer Sir Gordon Russell who, more than seventy years ago, wrote in a pamphlet entitled *Honesty and the Crafts – a Plea for a Broader Outlook*: 'Is there indeed so great a gulf between the faking of houses and furniture, and the faking of £5 notes? Are we to admire things because they are beautiful or because they are old?' Makepeace adopts a similar stance: 'When people come to Parnham and ask me if we make antiques, I say no. The only antiques we make are the antiques of the future.'

The intriguing visual illusion in hard materials of a 'cushion', knotted to a frame, makes a compelling creative statement. Originally the Knot Chair was designed for an American collector who considered the Artist's Prototype (shown here) too pale and haunting an image and requested the chair to be oiled to create a warm dark brown colour.

The frame of legs and arms is in English oak; the knotted seat and back in burr elm. All the handcarving was done in the John Makepeace Furniture Studio. The piece shows that comfort requires shape to encourage good posture, not soft surfaces.

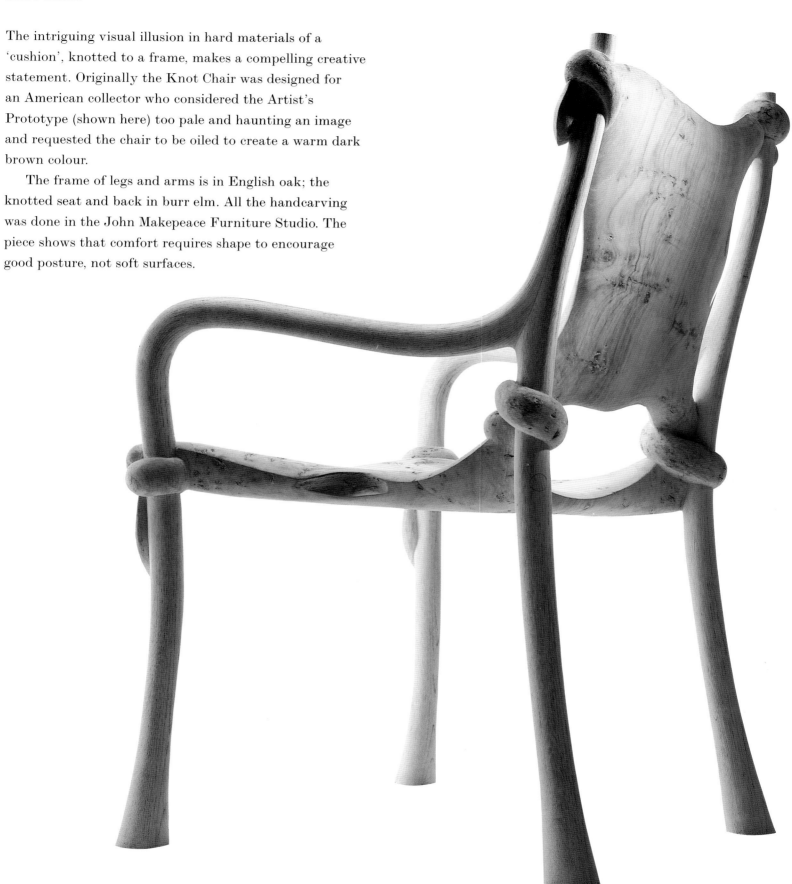

Left and right: *The Petra Serving Table has horizontal lines of burr oak acting as the mortar between blocks of solid burr elm. The soft grain has been ground away on all the vertical surfaces to give prominence to the knots of the wood. This piece encapsulates Prudence Glynn's remark that Makepeace feels about wood as jewellers feel about gold.*

John Makepeace has a special affinity with the art and craft of architecture, not simply for its own sake but because it can be used in an emblematic way to influence the lives of people living and working together.

While he restored the ancient halls of Parnham House to create a cohesive artistic centre, his quest to establish a second creative community, deep in the woodlands at Hooke Park, has led to the development of a pioneering new architecture sculpted from the discarded thinnings of the forest. The buildings at Hooke Park represent an audacious bid to reunite structure and nature, engineering and biology 150 years after industrialization forced them apart. The unusual aesthetic that results is a direct response to the needs of ecology.

Makepeace believes that buildings are important not just for their abstract form-giving or place-making qualities but because of their effect on the people who use them. Architecture helps to shape individual behaviour and aspirations, yet its power as a profound influence on the human spirit is often overlooked.

As a small child, living at Fairfield and the Woad House, he was aware of his own architectural surroundings, and as he grew up his interest in buildings deepened. While still a teenager he made a trip to Salzburg in Austria to see the churches of the liturgical movement. Converted from farm buildings, they were simple, even minimalist, structures but vigorously expressive, and they offered a striking contrast to the Baroque churches which he later visited in southern Germany, and to Le Corbusier's magnificent Ronchamp Chapel in north-eastern France, which he studied in photographs.

Although Makepeace dismisses his early awakening to architecture as largely uncritical, one important aspect nevertheless took hold in his mind: 'All the buildings which attracted me were symbols of different philosophies and attitudes – powerful statements. That is what I began to look for in architecture as my interest in the subject developed.'

Previous page: An Andy Goldsworthy sculpture stands at the entrance to Hooke Park. Its artful use of a material most people would consider fit only for firewood is an apt symbol of Hooke Park's aim of environmental regeneration. Its circular form reflects the holistic relationship between forest, architecture and industry on the site.

Right: A student project to build a suspension bridge across a gully between the Prototype House and the Training Centre, using the natural resources of Hooke Park.

By the early 1960s Makepeace had become an enthusiastic student of building construction techniques, reading widely on the subject and observing work on sites wherever he could. On a philosophical level he began to see that architecture could define a complete way of living.

During the period at the start of the 1970s, when he concentrated on working with architects on interior contracts such as the Oxford Centre for Management Studies and Keble College in Oxford, his focus on buildings and interiors intensified. Significantly, his major collaborator then, ABK, was to be responsible for the first manifestations of a new organic building style at Hooke Park.

A significant event for Makepeace at that time was the award of a Gold Medal by the Royal Institute of British Architects to the leading German organic architect, Frei Otto. Makepeace went along to hear him accept his prize in London. Otto had made an international name for himself by creating a new architecture based on the study of tensile structures in the natural world. His German Pavilion at the 1967 Montreal Expo and his 1972 Munich Olympic Stadium, designed with Benisch and Partners, introduced a form of bio-architecture which derived from the spider's web and rejected the set-square used by the Modernists.

Otto's work represented for many in architecture a healing of the schism between nature and structure, biology and engineering, which had widened progressively since the Industrial Revolution. As the leading academic on the subject, Professor James Gordon, has pointed out the traditional technological structures prior to industrialization were largely based on biology: not only were the materials, such as wood, rope and canvas, biological, but so were many of the structural forms. Widespread use of metals, and of machinery such as steam engines and railways, however, introduced a new language in building which created a gulf between the biologists and the engineers.

For Makepeace, wondering how to unite furniture, buildings and landscape in a sustainable holistic framework, Frei Otto's profoundly moral vision of ecological construction was a revelation. It would be more than ten years, however, before the aspiring craftsman and master architect would work together to unite nature and structure at Hooke Park.

The origins of the entire Hooke Park adventure can be traced back to John Makepeace's experiences during a week-long visit to the 3600-acre (1460-ha) forest at Longleat with Parnham students in 1979. It was the wettest week of the year and the Parnham party was forced to abandon a life under canvas to shelter in a nissan hut. Every day different visiting tutors led projects based on the creation of artefacts from an area of neglected coppice, and Makepeace noticed the ease and speed with which this new, freshly harvested material could be used. It seemed to him that the same might be true of thinnings from broad-leaved and conifer forests.

Longleat's head forester, John McHardy, who became a personal friend of Makepeace, brought the subject of forestry alive for him. He explained how small-diameter trees, removed as thinnings to allow selected trees to grow to maturity, no longer had any significant commercial value, even though they accounted for half of the annual forest crop. They were used primarily for firewood and pulp, despite their structural potential, which was demonstrated by the many practical applications like coppiced willow in baskets and the furniture devised by the students.

Right: *View through the rough-hewn structure of the Prototype House, with smaller thinnings used as rafters in tension and larger thinnings as compression members. The building demonstrates an alternative technology while revealing an asymmetric beauty rarely seen in Western architecture.*

The Longleat experience planted a seed in Makepeace's mind and made him think about new ways of exploiting the properties of timber. Since the eighteenth century scientists, engineers and technologists had been continually researching and creating glamorous new materials for use in manufacture, yet the renewable resource of timber, particularly small-diameter timber (also known as roundwood), had been largely ignored. At a time when industry faced an environmental crisis and needed to develop more sustainable patterns of production, could the forest hold the key to a better future? Makepeace and his trustees were keen to develop an industrial culture of manufacturing in wood as a logical companion to man's intervention in planting forests, and as part of a vision of creating a network of sustainable businesses within rural communities. The rarefied craftsman had come down from his pedestal and onto the factory floor, brimful with new ideas about the relationship between the natural environment and our material world.

In the early 1980s Makepeace began to investigate the forestry scene more closely, and in particular to examine whether a woodland design, research and development centre could be established to find new uses for forest thinnings up to 8 inches (203mm) in diameter. His idea was to train people to set up new entrepreneurial woodland industries and to demonstrate new uses for roundwood. Importantly, the buildings in this new centre would be constructed of local timber, using techniques which could serve as an exemplar for the whole experiment. The Forestry Commission's conservator for the south-west of England, Leslie Troup, advised on suitable sites for such a centre and every weekend John and Jennie Makepeace went to visit them. These trips were pleasant enough in themselves but nothing productive came of them.

In 1982, however, a powerful ally came to the aid of Makepeace's vision. Lord Tonypandy, the Speaker of the House of Commons, agreed to host a reception at the Speaker's House in Westminster. Makepeace was able to outline his thesis to half-a-dozen Government ministers. He wasted few words in stating the economic and environmental benefits of his case. Trees, he explained, are the world's most energy-efficient and renewable source of structural material. Trees conserve and convert the earth's primary source of energy – the sun – into structural material, and minimal further energy is required to turn them into building components and products.

He described how the neglect of woodlands was attributable to a lack of markets for small-diameter timber. If woodland industries could be established to make use of this abundant resource, then forests could be conserved and managed more effectively and rural employment created. A woodland factory making products from roundwood made economic sense: a forester could cut to precise demand, and haulage costs, a significant part of the price of unprocessed timber, could be kept to a minimum if the manufacturing centre was built right next to the forest. It was a thesis which chimed with the findings of the Countryside Commission and similar bodies.

Following the reception at the Speaker's House, the Secretary of State for Wales, Nicholas Edwards, expressed interest in the initiative, so the search for a suitable site switched to the Welsh countryside. Then Leslie Troup advised Makepeace that the Forestry Commission was selling off a portfolio of eleven woodlands for £750,000, among them Hooke Park, a 330-acre (135-ha) mixed broad-leaved and conifer forest just four miles from Parnham House. As a mixed forest, Hooke Park had less commercial value than the ʻother woodlands. Nevertheless, the Parnham Trust, guided by Makepeace's instincts, tendered £250,000 for the site in 1983. There were no buildings on the land so the tender was made subject to outline planning approval. It was a generous and ultimately successful bid. Once again, the necessary fund-raising was a nail-biting affair. A Countryside Commission grant of £75,000 and £125,000 in donations helped the deal to go through, but the Parnham Trust still had a deficit of £50,000. The Forestry Commission agreed to the balance being paid over a four-year period. Makepeace was set to embark on the most profound architectural adventure of his career.

Above: *Internal views of the Prototype House showing its taut natural structure.*

Right: *Its external profile introduces a new organic vocabulary to the modern building.*

The woodland context of Hooke Park immediately evoked the work of Frei Otto. Otto's use of lightweight structures, and his ability to blend them with the natural environment, made his work wholly appropriate to Hooke's setting. A meeting was arranged with him at which Makepeace met the leading structural engineer Sir Edmund Happold, who had already worked in close collaboration with Otto.

Makepeace initially believed that Otto and Happold would be able to undertake the whole project between them. However, as Otto walked around the site discussing the concept, he decided that his own role should be that of consultant and that another architectural practice should be involved in the detailed resolution of the different buildings – workshops, housing, visitors' centre – which would eventually make up Hooke's rural campus. Richard Burton of ABK was therefore asked to join the design team. Not only had ABK played a significant part in Makepeace's career, and had had experience of designing university buildings, but Burton was a Parnham trustee and his two sons had trained at Parnham College. The idea of working alongside a world figure such as Frei Otto was an appealing one for him, as was the challenge of exploiting a construction material largely neglected for more than two centuries.

While Otto produced a range of options for the buildings in collaboration with the engineers in order to establish the potential of small roundwood and how best it could be used, Burton began to design the layout of the centre. Work focused on three basic themes: the tensioned structure, the arched structure and the simple compression structure. Burton recalls: 'We decided that it would be useful to study these while building. The students would then be living in the structures that they were learning about.'

The influential design critic Peter Dormer, a longtime supporter of the work at Hooke Park, has written: 'What changes a raw material into something valuable is human intelligence and creativity (as well, of course, as the inherent virtues of the resource). Timber has many virtues, including one that is often neglected – its great tensile strength.' Otto and Happold, a professor at Bath University, resolved to carry out a scientific analysis of the material to test its

structural properties. They focused on the strength of timber in tension: because of its immense strength, it could be used in smaller dimensions. That in turn prompted the question: how could such strength be best exploited? Normal mechanical methods of jointing in construction work were usually the source of weakness.

Science began to play a key role in the evolution of Hooke Park's new architecture. Material scientists at Bath University developed a method of achieving a strong, tensioned joint using epoxy resins and a substantial proportion of filler, with a threaded steel rod embedded in the resin to enable a connection to be made. A senior chemist at Imperial College advised on timber preservation treatments.

The first building to be constructed, the Prototype House, was built on a steep slope at Hooke Park in 1986-7. 'By that time,' says Makepeace, 'we had a good understanding of what was required to manage the forest. We had ascertained what trees could be thinned from the forest and had established that sixty per cent of the volume of thinnings could be converted into building components. It was astonishing to discover how well this natural resource could be used in construction.'

While Hooke Park forester Andrew Poore managed the timber crop, Makepeace orchestrated the dramatic process of innovation and experimentation proposed by Otto, Happold and ABK. He was determined to overcome a seemingly intractable problem: 'Talking to wood scientists, the common comment was that timber is so strong in tension that there is no means of testing it. And if you can't test it, you can't use it because you can't prove mathematically that it is satisfactory. It was a ridiculous bind to be in. Only by the inspired collaboration of three specialists – a world-class organic architect, an outstanding structural engineer and a rigorous modern design practice – could we find a way through.'

The Prototype House, which today is used for meetings and administration and as a refectory, introduced a new building vernacular. This was inspired directly by the woodland setting and the local crops of Norway spruce and Corsican pine. Peter Dormer describes the house as especially innovative: 'I suspect that Eastern cultures, the Japanese for example, will find the Hooke Park aesthetic easier to like because they have a tradition – in their pottery, for example – of seeing beauty in organic irregularity as well as in the dignity of man-made symmetry.'

The completion of the Prototype House coincided with the opening of Frei Otto's new factory for the furniture manufacturer Wilkhahn on a green field site in Germany. Otto had utilized Wilkhahn's own timber technology to create a series of lightweight wooden pavilions nestling in the landscape. The project was a stunning achievement. Together with the Prototype House, it reflected Happold's view that 'Otto has tied into his work his moral sense that man is part of nature, and has an obligation to live harmoniously with nature and to use resources efficiently'. As Otto himself argues, 'architects have been building against nature for five thousand years. It has been their duty to protect mankind against enemies, and especially against their greatest enemy – nature. Houses have been their weapons and their symbols of victory. We still build against nature. Our duty is not to destroy but to conserve. But have we recognized that task?'

The Prototype House – built at a cost of just £50,000 – was a symbol of harmony with nature, not victory over its forces. But if it represented one level of architectural risk-taking, then the construction of a second building at Hooke – the 6458-square-foot (600-sq-m) Training Centre – significantly upped the stakes.

The Bluebell Woods at Hooke Park. This ancient woodland has become the setting for an audacious experiment in reuniting nature with structure, biology with engineering. Its abundant crop of forest thinnings is an energy-efficient material which, when used for building components and furniture products, can create rural jobs and stimulate industry.

This was to be the main building on the site, a dramatic structure which would exploit the pliability of the thinnings and utilize their potential for compression and tension. It would provide the focus for walks and trails through the woodland, and allow public access to an observation gantry above the workshops. The realization of this strictly budgeted project was, however, intensely problematic. The contractors refused to work to a fixed price contract and the building had no precedent, so no quantity surveyor could give a price; the architects and engineers were journeying into uncharted territory. As a consequence, the final cost of the building overran considerably. 'The going got rough and it was a very significant learning experience.'

The use of a polymer fabric to cover the lattice-shell roof was challenged by some critics of the scheme, who argued that this undermined its ecological credibility. But Makepeace responded that new organic architecture needed to be developed stage by stage, and that the main focus of the Centre was the experimental bending of softwoods to span space. Fundamentally, the structure is composed of compressed arches made from long, wet roundwood. It thus provides an apt architectural symbol for everything that the Parnham Trust is trying to achieve at Hooke Park.

Makepeace acknowledges the important part played by Frei Otto in the resolution of a building which has been the subject of discussion in architectural magazines all over the world: 'Frei has a capacity to recognize simple truths, to work with them, and to generate dynamic and lively results.' Sir Edmund Happold – an engineer who has been on the receiving end of a great many fanciful architectural schemes – adds: 'Frei's great strength is that he sits down to something, works on it until he understands it. Unlike many architects, he does not think that all you have to do is want something, therefore you create it and it will come right.'

The combination of basic forestry and carpentry skills with the deceptively simple jointing and structural technology used to build the Training Centre broke new ground in construction techniques using renewable resources. The building gave Makepeace a recognizable emblem to carry on his crusade through the corridors of power.

Significantly in 1990, the year in which the Training Centre was completed, Britain imported ninety per cent of all its timber and timber products, representing a net loss to the economy of £7 billion, and the demographic outlook for the decade predicted the loss of some 100,000 agricultural jobs by the year 1999.

Previous pages: *The Training Centre in skeletal form during construction with compressed timber arches exposed to the elements, and in its finished state complete with polymer fabric roof which enhances the building's anthropomorphic image. Despite its traumatic development, as the architects made a journey into the unknown and budgets overran, the Training Centre has attracted worldwide publicity for its pioneering approach.*

Right: *Inside the Training Centre. Beneath an organic roofline the main workshop occupies a vast womb-like space, a hive of industry in developing new skills, technologies, products and markets for forest thinnings.*

A further symbol of the aims of the Parnham Trust is provided by Andy Goldsworthy's circular sculptures at the entrance to Hooke Park. This work was commissioned in 1987, after the completion of the Prototype House, and sponsored by Common Ground, a body dedicated to promoting community involvement in the arts and the environment, and South-West Arts, the local regional arts authority. Goldsworthy created his sculptures from second-grade timber which had grown on a hillside where the land had been slipping for many years; the trees had bent to compensate. Such material would have been considered by most people to be fit only for firewood – but Goldsworthy had other ideas. As Makepeace says, 'No material is inferior. It is just better for some uses than for others.'

Hooke Park's innovative architecture provides the framework for a second creative community, a second exercise in social engineering, but Makepeace confesses that he has found the path less smooth than at Parnham: 'At Parnham, everything went according to plan, but Hooke is a larger, altogether more complex enterprise. Its pioneering nature attracts support from the private sector but we have been reliant on Government and European Community funding for revenue. It is ahead of its time and is still in its infancy. But already it has influenced professionals in many aspects of design and ecology, and in the developing world. It has directly inspired many other buildings.'

Hooke Park has already implemented a number of pioneering educational initiatives. Now it is focusing on the research and development of housing systems; the prototypes will provide residential accommodation for two-year courses, summer courses and visits by schools and special interest groups. By the new millennium – less than twenty years since first acquiring the site – the Parnham Trust also hopes to have opened a new visitors' centre at Hooke Park as part of its campaign to educate the public about the value of small-diameter forest thinnings in building construction.

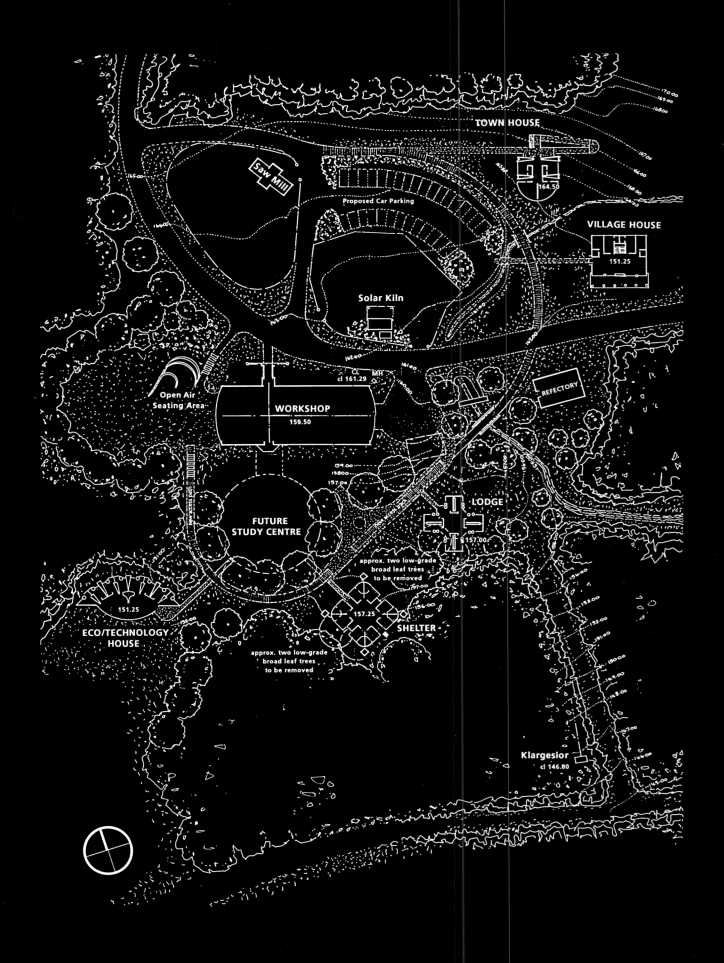

The idea of a residential college on the site remains firmly in John Makepeace's sights. To achieve this requires the building of accommodation for students, tutors and visitors at Hooke Park. So the great architectural adventure continues with the Houses at Hooke project, led by British architect Edward Cullinan.

The Training Centre at Hooke Park is not a structure that can be reproduced elsewhere but it is Makepeace's intention that it will be possible to replicate the Houses at Hooke. The aim is to use timber thinnings to create five distinct housing types, which will be built on the site as exemplars capable of being adopted in a range of different contexts. The cost of the houses is estimated at £600,000 and a major fund-raising drive is under way. The Department of the Environment, which is very interested in this unique form of building research, has pledged £150,000 for research. Only when there are five houses and a visitor centre on the site, providing shelter from the elements and demonstrating the structural properties of roundwood, can Makepeace's vision of a financially unassailable and globally respected research and training establishment at Hooke Park be fully realized. The houses are due for completion in 1997.

Makepeace interviewed five architects before appointing Edward Cullinan, who is renowned for the skilful integration of old and new in his work. 'His buildings have a poetry which is rare', comments Makepeace. 'He has a good feeling for housing and is sensitive to working on a small scale.' Cullinan has so far proposed five designs for houses at Hooke Park. The first is a lodge, which could provide holiday accommodation in a forest or a national park. Currently such buildings, often log cabins imported from Scandinavia, take a boxlike form inappropriate to a sensitive landscape site. The lodge will have an organic framework made from forest thinnings and its roof will be turfed and covered in plants; internally there will be a central space for student seminars with study-bedrooms on each side. The second house is a simple shelter, a circular, earth-hugging structure, again using forest thinnings under tension to achieve curved forms. This building type could serve as crisis housing after a flood or famine. It is envisaged that the shelter will house

Left: *Map showing the Hooke Park of tomorrow: an integrated research, design and development campus with the Houses at Hooke providing staff and student accommodation, and a new Study Centre forming a focal point on the site.*

Below: *The Hooke Park campus shown in relation to Hooke Park itself, the 330-acre (133-ha) forest owned by the Parnham Trust, and surrounding terrain.*

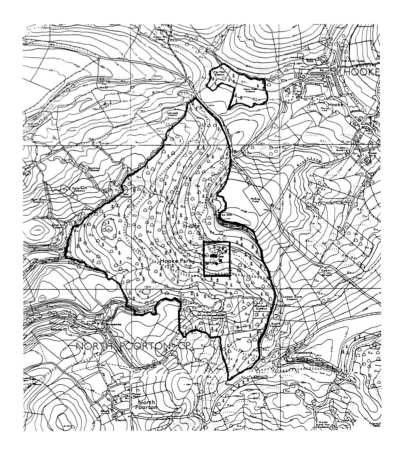

THE LODGE

Forest thinnings are utilized to create a simple partition-and-skin structure, with eight study-bedrooms opening onto a central meeting area in which shared facilities can be grouped.

A SIMPLE SHELTER

An earth-hugging structure with simple spans tied down at four corners like a tent. This shelter has been developed for crisis accommodation or for use in the developing world.

VILLAGE HOUSE

A two-storey structure with a gracefully arched roofline, the Village House is constructed using round-wood poles. The building envelope can be used as a family home for a resident tutor on the ground floor, with accommodation above for visitors.

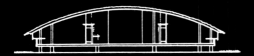

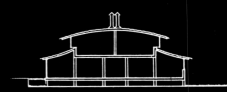

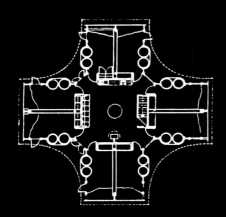

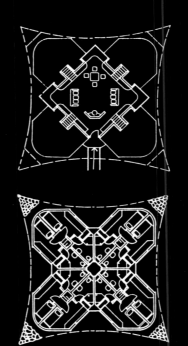

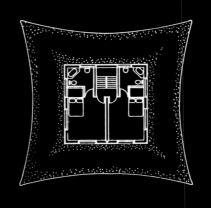

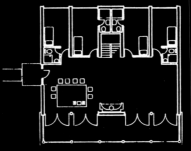

ECOLOGY/TECHNOLOGY HOUSE

A more sophisticated use of solar and water-recycling technology is a feature of this design, which has student rooms fanning out from a common room.

TOWN HOUSE

A town house with convex curved party walls and upper floor overhang, which utilizes the wood technology of Hooke Park. It is intended to provide the construction industry with a repeatable model for a starter home.

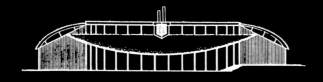

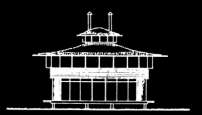

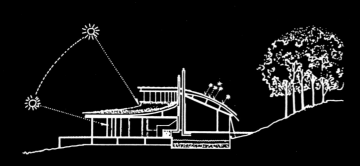

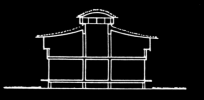

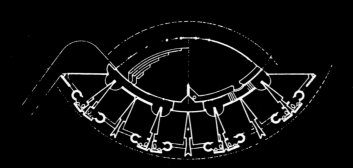

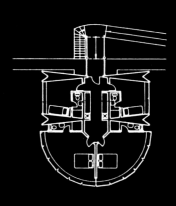

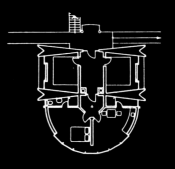

eight study-bedrooms at Hooke Park. The third house is a two-storey village house, whose gracefully arched roof line has been achieved by means of roundwood poles. The fourth design is a technologically more sophisticated building for executive use. Directed towards the sun, it will employ solar energy, heat retention and waste-recycling techniques. The fifth is a town house, an ecological version of a starter home, with an overhanging upper floor to provide additional space as well as protection from the weather. 'These designs are outline proposals', says Makepeace. 'They must be price-conscious and repeatable. Tough decisions must be made, but Cullinan's capacity for poetry in design will shine through these constraints.'

The building of the Houses at Hooke will go a long way to realizing Makepeace's dream of a second creative community – one which unites designers and ecologists with building technologists and scientists engaged in the study of sustainable new materials. It will also embrace research, education, forestry and manufacture on a single site which is open to the public. For Makepeace, the art of architecture remains the art of the possible. 'I have always felt', he reflects, 'that had I other lives, architecture would be one of them. But my designs would always start from the inside, and exterior form would be an expression of interior use.'

EDUCATIONAL PROGRAMMES

The educational initiative set up by the Parnham Trust at Hooke Park is envisaged as a foil to Parnham in cultural and philosophical terms. Whereas Parnham's focus is on teaching the individual the skills required to be self-sufficient as a craft maker, Hooke Park's prime concern is to encourage the creation of a new industrial culture which will make expert use of forest thinnings for building components and products. Hooke Park also aims to be more globally significant in terms of stimulating environmental and economic ways forward for forestry.

Makepeace's aspirations as an educationalist have grown from a desire to direct the training of craftsmen towards an even more ambitious objective – to affect the way in which entire patterns of industry are to evolve in the future. He is making a quantum leap and it could be argued that the mixed fortunes of the initial educational programmes at Hooke reflect the enormity of the task still confronting him. As an educational centre, Hooke has demonstrated the significance of its role, but its income is reliant on the completion of its facilities. Nevertheless, there have been some notable advances which add to Makepeace's credentials as a pioneering teacher. Since 1983, when Hooke Park was acquired by the Parnham Trust, two major educational programmes have been run as pilot schemes, preceded by a series of six-month courses which concentrated on basic woodworking skills and forestry management for local unemployed people.

The first programme ran for three years, from 1989 to 1991, and trained seventy-two short-course and twenty-four full-time students. It was funded by the European Social Fund, the Department of Employment and two local authorities. Its aim was to give graduates a foundation in practical skills across a range of disciplines – design, production, management and marketing – so that they could establish their own rural businesses in design and manufacture using indigenous timber resources. High levels of rural unemployment are not unique to Britain; they are a feature right across Europe, which explains the interest of the European Community in Makepeace's initiative to revitalize woodland industries.

Trannon is an example of a furniture-making company which has built a successful rural business as a direct result of the Hooke Park initiative and is dedicated to making furniture using forest thinnings. The company was set up by Hooke's design tutor David Colwell, who in 1991 was joined by two students – Roy Tam and Richard Foyle.

By targeting the contract market in particular, Trannon has been able to avoid the pitfalls of many furniture designer-makers tied exclusively to retail and domestic clients. Highly visible commissions from museums and galleries have been especially useful in building a profile for the company, which has its main workshop at Wilton, near Salisbury, and its design studio and prototyping facilities in central Wales.

'Trannon has high standards of design and manufacture, and represents just the right kind of industry for the resource,' says John Makepeace. 'The contract market entails producing in larger volumes than for individual pieces, but this is not mass manufacture. It would be too hard to source the thinnings.'

For Roy Tam, who studied industrial design engineering at the Royal College of Art a decade before joining the Hooke Park course, the experience was 'an intensely practical one' which he describes as 'an experiment in the fundamentals'. Trannon's expertise in design and manufacture using forest thinnings is set to extend beyond Britain: the company is developing new markets in Europe and the United States.

Trannon Furniture's C3 Stacking Chair in steambent ash thinnings with birch ply seat, designed by David Colwell. This version with its drill holes was a special edition developed for use in the café and library of the Crafts Council headquarters in Islington, London.

MALCOLM STRONG

Malcolm Strong trained as a fuel and combustion scientist. He worked for a number of years in the oil industry before joining the Hooke Park course in 1989. Today he runs his own business, designing and making footbridges in Perthshire, Scotland.

'I was trained to think in terms of fuel and energy consumption,' he says. 'Hooke Park College gave me the opportunity to delve into timber and address serious environmental issues. It was full of radical intent, an open workshop with influences coming from all kinds of directions, not least the woodland itself.'

While at Hooke, Strong experimented with the development of an innovative footbridge, using forest thinnings in a decking structure connected by steel pins to form a flat chain, which is converted into a curved truss by compressed arches. 'I learnt that if you have good design, you don't need a huge capital investment,' he says.

Since moving to Battleby, Perth, in spring 1992 and setting up his own business, Strong has developed. He makes a range of footbridges, from those with a 3ft (1m) span for flatpack sale to private customers in garden centres to others with a 60ft (20m) span commissioned by local authorities.

His footbridges use European larch and Douglas Fir grown in north-eastern Scotland. This is one reason why Strong has received support and encouragement from Scottish Natural Heritage, which has a remit to conserve natural Scotland. 'My competitors import Scandinavian or tropical hardwoods,' says Strong, 'but I use home-grown timber.'

Elegant footbridge at Hooke Park, designed and made by Malcolm Strong using small-dimension timber of the type normally reserved only for fence posts. The project was a prototype which Strong later developed into a range of footbridge products made of thinnings.

The programme was directed by mechanical engineer John Eden. It was thoroughly entrepreneurial, focusing on research into the location and properties of the timber to be used, analyzing its structural and manufacturing potential and studying logical sites for woodland businesses. The courses generated significant new business as well as products which showed the potential of forest thinnings.

'Hooke's graduates are now dispersed all over the UK, working with forests and local woodlands', says Makepeace. 'The school at Hooke has a far broader economic potential than Parnham.' Hooke graduates have indeed used their training to go in many different directions. Jim Marston, for example, has produced bent green ash bowls which have sold well internationally in designer stores. Malcolm Strong has specialized in making bridges for sensitive landscapes for Scottish Heritage. And, in perhaps the most power- ful reflection of the course's purpose, two former Hooke students, Roy Tam and Richard Foyle, have teamed up with their design tutor, David Colwell, to form Trannon Furniture, which manufactures quality products using for- est thinnings. Roy Tam, who graduated from Hooke Park in 1991, described the training 'as very hands-on compared to other furniture courses. There was a slow start as we watched the workshops being built and the inevitable clash of personalities because the people on the course were hand-picked to make a lot of life-changing decisions. But wonderful friendships developed and we set up our company while we were still on the course – which demonstrates its entrepreneurial focus.'

The second programme at Hooke Park ran for two years, from 1992 to 1994, latterly under the direction of Peter Miles, a former furniture manufacturer. It consisted of two one-year courses and had broadly the same objectives as the first programme. Again, the initiative spawned new busi- nesses and new products. According to Simon Burvill, who studied at Hooke in 1992 before setting up a garden furni- ture business with Christian Gaze, a Parnham graduate, 'The setting was fabulous. When you are working in wood, it is great to be totally surrounded by it. But you needed to be very self-reliant and to know what you wanted to get out of the course at Hooke.'

GAZE BURVILL

The Hampshire-based garden-furniture company Gaze Burvill is a unique collaboration between a graduate of Hooke Parke, Simon Burvill, and a graduate of Parnham College, Christian Gaze. They joined forces to launch their company in February 1993, swiftly widening the client base for their well-made steambent English oak products from private individuals to local authorities.

Burvill went to Hooke Park in 1992 as an engineering graduate who had worked in export and marketing, and who played with woodworking as a hobby. Gaze, meanwhile, arrived at Parnham with a well-travelled background which included a stint working on the oil rigs in Texas. As Gaze remarks: 'Simon and I mask each other's failings. Any new venture is a gamble. We take such a different approach to problems that we have a better chance of getting it right together.'

John Makepeace describes the partnership as an especially good one. 'Both were mature students. Christian was a designer who tended to overreach aesthetically. Simon was commercially experienced, a good communicator, but with little design confidence. It was clever and appropriate of Gaze Burvill to go into garden furniture. The products avoid any overriding sense of joinery and mechanical woodworking.'

Court Seat designed and made by Gaze Burvill in steambent English oak.

A range of bowls, clocks and ashtrays in Norway spruce with alcohol-based coloured staining by John Russell-Sanders, a Hooke Park graduate in 1991.

John Russell-Sanders differed from many of the first Hooke Park students in that he had already received a traditional apprenticeship as a carpenter. His return to study at Hooke Park, having left the industry for a time and worked in the music and advertising worlds, thus developed his existing skills within a new philosophical framework.

'The course was radical and different. There was a belief that you could change things,' says Russell-Sanders. During his time at Hooke Park he developed an artistic range of clocks, bowls and ash trays in Norway spruce, cleverly using brightly coloured stains to disguise the low-grade nature of the timber. He also developed a flatpack chair in spruce for sale through the Victoria & Albert Museum.

On leaving Hooke Park, Russell-Sanders shared a workshop with Trannon Furniture, run by fellow alumni, but today he has his own premises and employs his own staff. He has built part of his business on a spectacular programme of restoration in oak – doors, windows, panelling, bridges and boathouses – for a twelfth-century priory in Somerset owned by the theatrical producer Cameron Mackintosh. He also works with clients in France and Jersey.

CLAIRE RICHTER

Claire Richter worked in marketing for J. C. Case, the American tractor company, and managed a shop selling Welsh knitwear before deciding to set up her own business. She went to study at Hooke Park in 1989 in order to understand and control the entire process of product development and manufacture.

While at Hooke, she developed prototypes for a range of woodblock flooring using beech, oak and ash thinnings. Her work demonstrated that even the most stylish interior decor products could be created using the abundant natural resource of the Hooke Park woodlands.

'I enjoyed my time there,' she recalls, 'but I think the best is yet to come for Hooke. When the site is more fully developed with student accommodation, then it will be a wonderful place to develop new products.'

Ash-block Forest Flooring made from forest thinnings by Claire Richter, a Hooke Park graduate in 1990.

JIM MARSTON

Jim Marston lives and works in Dorset, close to both Parnham House and Hooke Park. His business – designing and making delicate ash bowls and baskets – reflects his time spent developing new techniques as one of Hooke Park's first students from 1989 to 1990.

Marston had studied furniture design at Leeds Polytechnic before arriving at Hooke Park. He describes the course as 'a strange woodworking monastery deep in the forest. It was a time of experiment, it was brilliant.'

Today Marston sells his products in leading British retail outlets such as The Conran Shop and Heal's, as well as the Parnham House shop. His work is also available in New York, Paris and Tokyo. His bowl-making technique is based on repeatedly machining the material into thin sheets. 'It's like working in a bakery,' he explains, 'with lots of little pieces of wood in trays. It's all very basic – lacquer is wiped on with radiator rollers on sticks.'

Despite the improvisatory nature of his own work, Marston is clear about the contribution of Hooke Park: 'Woodworking has a low perceived value compared to something like silversmithing. When you see what other Hooke graduates have achieved, it helps to raise the image.'

Arc bowls and baskets in ash, designed and made by Jim Marston, a Hooke Park graduate in 1990.

For Norwegian-American designer Petter Southall, Hooke Park was 'a place to initiate your business plans, a place to realize what you always wanted to do in woodland industry'. He arrived in Dorset having spent nearly a decade building boats in Norway, six years travelling the world and one year studying with cabinet maker James Krenov in California.

Southall only discovered Hooke Park College through a chance meeting in a pub, but on such random encounters are careers changed. Today he runs his own furniture-making business at Chilcombe in Dorset, creating pieces to commission for galleries, corporations and private individuals. He works only in English oak, exploiting its properties in a subtle and intelligent way.

'My business is not as closely linked today to forestry management as when I first envisaged it,' says Southall, 'but Hooke Park taught me a great deal by touching on so many trades - design, manufacture in wood, business management.'

Side Table in thin-dimension oak with coldbent legs, designed and made by Petter Southall, a Hooke Park graduate in 1990.

Funding for this particular programme at Hooke Park was provided by the Department of Employment. Twenty-two students were admitted to each course. In the second year, run in collaboration with Bournemouth University, all twenty-two students gained their MSc in Forest Product Technology (Design and Manufacture). Try as it might, however, Hooke Park could not emulate the intense academic and practical focus of Parnham. There were essential differences which made it impossible. Unlike the residential Parnham students, who could concentrate fully on their work, Hooke Park students had no accommodation on the site. And Parnham was a private, totally independent college whereas the initial educational programmes at Hooke depended on external funding. An additional problem was presented by the fact that the course required by Bournemouth University placed a good deal of emphasis on an academic thesis, whereas the Trust's goals are largely pragmatic and entrepreneurial. It was therefore decided to launch future courses only when Hooke Park could offer residential facilities for fee-paying students and for staff and research fellows. The Trust is giving this accommodation urgent priority.

Despite its teething problems, Makepeace remains as committed as ever to the educational mission at Hooke Park. With the building of the Prototype House and the Training Centre the Trust has made a valuable case to the construction industry, and, through regular woodland surveys, Hooke Park has demonstrated the beneficial effects on flora and fauna of forest management which allows light onto the forest floor. Now he is excited at what the Houses at Hooke programme will reveal. 'In educational terms, the territory at Parnham College is well trodden', he explains. 'But at Hooke Park we are conducting blue-sky research. Hooke's future students will play an important role in the process of exploration.

Shona Mackie's series of seven paintings which hang in Parnham House, depicting the development of Hooke Park.

A HOLISTIC VISION

If the environmental focus of Hooke Park is to complete the circle in John Makepeace's life, giving a sense of unity and completeness to a designer who had been unable to forge connecting links in life until he took up a career in the crafts, then the ring is not yet complete. Hooke Park is still at a formative stage. It is a larger, more complex and more experimental enterprise than Parnham, and more dependent on external forces than the tight-knit creative craft guild at the ancient house over which Makepeace exercises total control.

There is no doubt, however, that Hooke Park brings an extra dimension to an understanding of John Makepeace as a designer and as a person. Its spirit of ecology underscores the natural forms that recur in his furniture. Its focus on woodland design, manufacture and management is a reprise of the conceptual, technical and entrepreneurial skills which knit together the curriculum at Parnham College. And its emphasis on an under-utilized forest crop offers a counterbalance to the unabashed luxury of the high-value furniture made in his Studio workshop.

A set of seven paintings hangs in Parnham House, the work of young British artist and illustrator Shona Mackie, portraying the sequence of events and the facilitating elements behind the establishment of Hooke Park: the Parnham Trust which directs the whole enterprise, the planting of seeds, the harvesting of the woodland crop, the programme of conservation, the raising of funds, the process of design, and finally the construction of buildings. There is in this sequence a strong sense of the holistic vision that informs John Makepeace's life and work. But in the search for connections and completeness, Makepeace recognizes that his journey of self-discovery is far from over.

As John Makepeace looks to the future, he believes that handcrafted objects will not be sidelined by the progress of technology but will be exalted for their tangible representation of human values and sensibilities. He regards his own approach not as retreating from the problems of industry but as suggesting alternative models of production which combine sustainable development with individual responsibility.

Parnham House and Hooke Park have already contributed major initiatives to the international search for new solutions to current ecological and social problems. They are set to play an even more prominent role in the future as Makepeace seeks new goals for his creative and environmental vision.

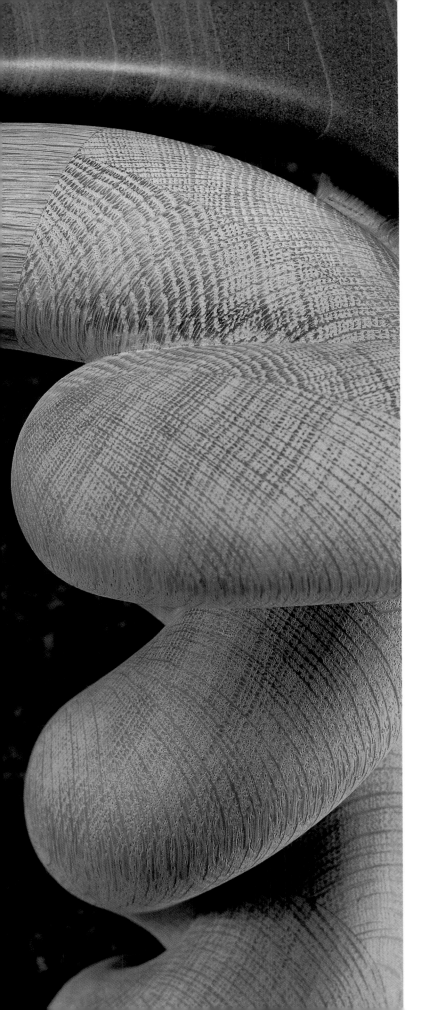

As we approach the new millennium it becomes clear that in their wide scope John Makepeace's activities represent both a retreat from manufacturing industry, in the emphasis on handmade objects at Parnham, and a sustainable alternative to it, in the work at Hooke Park. His outlook and ideas have attracted the interest of large numbers of young people precisely because mainstream industry remains unattractive to many of those starting a career. Makepeace's message is that only when the concept of manufacturing is connected more clearly to underlying social idealism can the energies of young people be properly marshalled to create a better world. This passionate belief evidently strikes a vibrant chord in those who choose to train under him, work with him or contribute funds to his initiatives.

In view of the threat which now faces the natural world, the best way to start a process of uniting industry with social ethics is by focusing on the environment, says Makepeace: 'The environment will be the major catalyst for mobilizing the idealism of the next generation. So far the ecological debate has predominantly been about abuse of our natural systems, about the negativity of waste and pollution. The next stage will be more constructive as we look for positive environmental measures from industry.'

How industry responds will determine the innovations of tomorrow. Whatever happens, these are likely to be very different from today's conventional scientific and market advances. Makepeace envisages that technology and craft will not only coexist but will be mutually supportive. In that case, the artist-craftsman will have an important role to play into the next century. 'Designer-makers who are not tied to industrial processes or to serving large markets are a valuable stimulus to industry. Their role will be to use their work to explore the full potential of artefacts as vehicles for artistic expression in an aesthetically progressive and demanding sector of the market.'

Indeed, it could be argued that the lovingly handcrafted chair and handthrown pot will be celebrated by a society which craves the physical qualities of a well-made artefact in a world of virtual reality. Makepeace recognizes that the signature pieces of his Studio have the capacity to increase in importance and value, but suggests that opportunities for future innovation are open to exponents of every medium: 'Whether craftsmen or computer software engineers, we are all creating symbols. We are all embracing semiotics of one kind or another. What are pieces of craft furniture but signals for the designer, the maker and the user? Virtual Reality is also about semiotics. In that sense, we speak the same language.'

This argument, however, only applies to the symbolic significance of the object. Beyond that, the physical dimension of handmade furniture, for example, provides tangible evidence of our values as a society in a form which will survive far beyond the last fading blips of a computer screen. In the same way that graphic designers are reviving traditional techniques such as hot metal type, or scratching calligraphy on sheets of vellum to escape the relentless momentum of the digital revolution, so craft furniture satisfies an inner need. Makepeace recognizes within his own work and within the work of those he trains that 'a significant part of our being needs to be sustained by tangible objects which enrich our sensibilities'.

However, he is resistant to the idea of being branded an escapee from the tyranny of the machine, a Luddite whose answer to the inexorable advances of the industrial society is to get back to the woods. This is evident, for example, in his interest in advanced aerospace engineering and the fact that he draws some of his structural design inspiration from that field. He also sees new technology as a liberating rather than an oppressive force in many contexts. 'I am not retreating from the industrial world,' he argues, 'I am simply looking for an alternative way forward.'

Makepeace's understanding of William Morris perhaps holds a key to his seemingly contradictory urges. Morris was the figurehead of the Arts and Crafts Movement, which so captured his imagination as a teenager seeking direction and meaning in his life. The observation by Morris in the midst of the Industrial Revolution, that any improvement in the work men do rapidly and inevitably leads to an improvement in the men who do it, influenced Makepeace profoundly, just as it had influenced the English furniture pioneer Sir Gordon Russell before him.

But whereas Russell became frustrated by the anti-industrial philosophy of the Arts and Crafts Movement, arguing that only the children of wealthy factory owners could afford to live in the way that it advocated, Makepeace has remained true to Morris's original spirit. Whereas Russell marched into mass manufacturing in the 1930s, making Murphy radio cabinets in their tens of thousands (his surviving company is today part of a multi-national group), Makepeace has kept his rural workshop small and independent, and has retained purist craft ideals.

John Makepeace does not, however, want to turn the clock back to the early nineteenth century. In fact he argues: 'Only now is it possible really to understand and achieve William Morris's vision for society. When he talked about making work more meaningful for people, he was a hundred years ahead of his time. The key to improving quality of work lies with the technological revolution we are now experiencing, not the industrial one which tied people to a production line. Morris may have had an over-glamorous view of medieval England but this gave him a sense of the future. He was extraordinarily perceptive.'

Morris was also an environmentalist ahead of his time. 'He was instrumental in setting up the National Trust, he was aware of the damage being done to the environment,' enthuses Makepeace, 'but once you understand that nature is inherently renewable, then you can have industry which uses renewable resources and you don't need to reject industry outright. William Morris was on the verge of grasping that. I like to think that if he was alive today he would play an active role in the Parnham Trust.'

Left: *Detail from a washed oak and slate table.*

Previous page: *Handcarved pattern on a Ziggurat oak plinth. John Makepeace argues that his craft focus is not trying to turn the clock back; instead it is suggesting alternative ways forward.*

ZIGGURAT LOW TABLE

This piece was specially designed to sit in the all-white upholstered room of a private London collector. It takes its inspiration from a Julian Schnabel painting with which it shares the space, and reflects Makepeace's more recent fascination with ethnic pattern-carving.

A glass top within a frame of pale scrubbed oak sits above fourteen oak plinths, or columns. These feature a number of different patterns carved into wide boards of English oak, which were originally planted at Longleat in Hampshire in 1760.

A combination of hand and machine techniques was used to carve the plinths: at the corners, where the four vertical surfaces of the plinth are joined, the carved texture is mirrored from one section to the next. Makepeace's aim with the piece was not only to respond to the very specific and heightened artistic and architectural setting of the client, but also to bring a sense of three-dimensionality to the surface patterning of solid wood.

As a testimony to the successful way this has been achieved, Makepeace's Ziggurat plinth was chosen as a fine example of contemporary wood carving by the British Crafts Council for its 1994 touring exhibition, *The Woodcarver's Craft*.

Makepeace's view of the future for the Parnham Trust reflects the restlessness of the visionary who remains eager to conquer new worlds and extend communication between nature, furniture, buildings, industry and technology. Despite the small scale of his 'cells of excellence', he is determined to drive all his activities up to a higher level in terms of international recognition. Wherever there is a new opportunity, he is determined to exploit it. Wherever there is already a record of achievement, he envisages further challenges. Makepeace is the complete radical in his refusal to stand still and in his endless appetite for revolution.

He has set himself demanding goals for the future. In particular he wants to raise the profile of his work in the Far East. Having established the American Friends of Parnham, Makepeace envisages a similar organization to act as his flagship among the 'tiger economies' of the East.

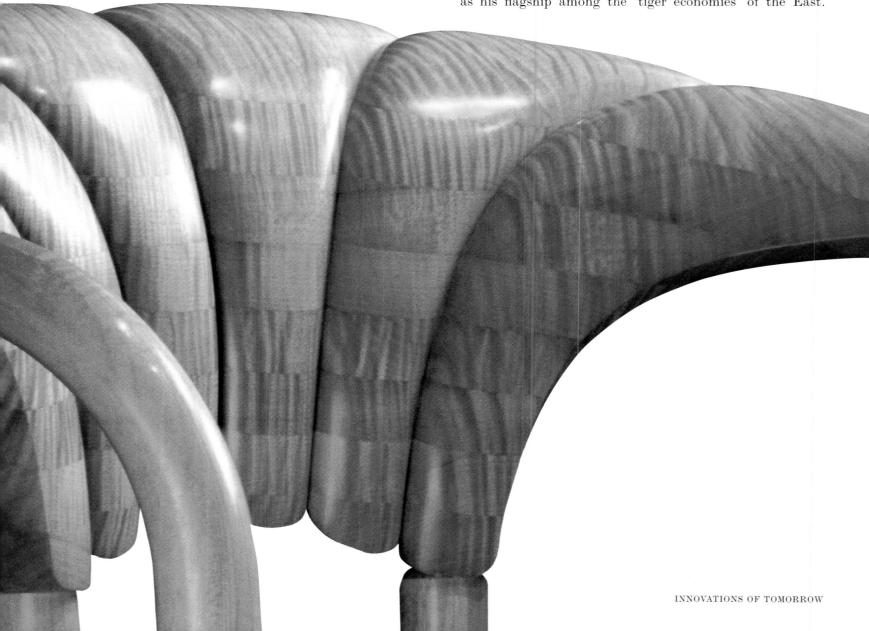

Already Japanese students have been to Parnham on a summer tour as a stepping stone to an exchange programme between Parnham alumni and apprentices in craft workshops in Japan. In the longer term Makepeace would like to see Japanese students on the residential course at Parnham. 'There is a sea change taking place in Japanese culture, and a number of their craft businesses are keen to assimilate Western influences', he observes.

Underlying his fascination with Pacific Asia is a concern that the current shift in wealth creation to the other side of the world will result in an exodus from Europe of research and development expertise and funding. 'A key question is what will be the future for Europe', says Makepeace. 'The idea that European countries will be niche centres for advanced research and technologies, while the Far East concentrates on mass manufacturing, could be undermined if the research follows the wealth creation. That is what could happen.'

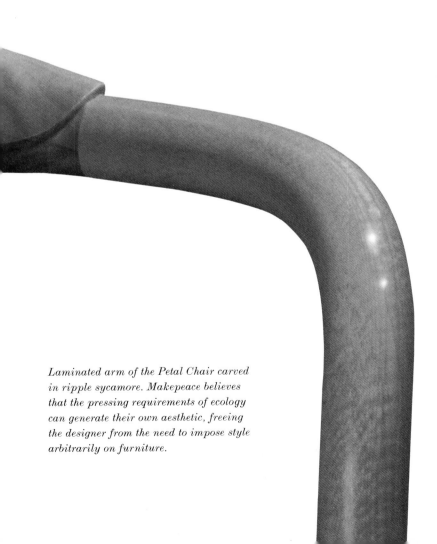

Laminated arm of the Petal Chair carved in ripple sycamore. Makepeace believes that the pressing requirements of ecology can generate their own aesthetic, freeing the designer from the need to impose style arbitrarily on furniture.

Business forecasts have identified high quality art and design-based European businesses as having a bright future in tomorrow's global economy. 'But', Makepeace explains, 'these businesses, including my own, clearly need to develop a part of their market outside Europe.' Encouragingly for him, his vision of ecologically responsible industry embracing sensitive craft values finds a ready audience in Japan, where aspects of his philosophy are reflected in the nation's cultural traditions.

His ambition to develop a market in Japan does not suggest any lessening of his interest in America, where he remains keen to widen his base. It is clear, however, that expansion into new international markets will have an impact on the furniture he makes from English hardwoods because of the diversity of climatic conditions around the world. Commissions from the American Mid-West, where the moisture content of timber is dramatically lower than in northern Europe, for instance, suggest an explanation for Makepeace's recent move towards veneered and curved surfaces connected by more muscular forms.

Once a self-reliant environmental and educational community is firmly established at Hooke Park, the Parnham Trust will be in a position to use Hooke and Parnham as key pieces in an operation involving educational exchanges, joint research and building projects, and technology transfer and consultancy schemes with organizations around the world. Makepeace sees the scale of his enterprises as a positive advantage because it allows him to be more radical in proposing solutions to global environmental problems through the efficient industrial use of a material that nature itself can provide. 'At Parnham we must encourage our alumni to recognize their abilities and leadership potential in order to develop successful workshops and employ and train a future generation of craft makers', he says. 'At Hooke Park we must work towards the generation of an entire network of sustainable businesses linked to our forests and woodlands.'

Natural form with structural integrity: the Web Table in olive ash, maple and burr elm combines the delicate and the muscular.

NEW AESTHETICS

The grand prize of this strategy is the creation of a new range of aesthetics generated by environmental and ethical considerations. This is inherent in the irregular, expressionist style of the new buildings at Hooke Park, with their use of tensioning and compression in doorways, entrances, walls and windows. As the critic Peter Dormer explains:

'What is fascinating is the effect such a project has upon aesthetic expectations. We are used in an industrial culture to neatness, perfection and order. Now the workshops at Hooke Park *do* present you with a kind of order but it is the order of asymmetry. There is a kind of perfection but it is organic, it is not regular. Thus one is looking at a very different kind of dynamic to those aesthetics which radical artists, designers and architects asserted earlier this century, such as De Stijl, Constructivism and Suprematism – which were basically the aesthetics of the panel and the 'I' beam or rectangle and line.'

The needs of ecology rather than the needs of the machine can indeed serve as a powerful modifier of the appearance of buildings and products. This idea echoes a campaign that the veteran American environmentalist and designer Victor Papanek has pursued since the publication of his book *Design for the Real World* in 1970. As recently as 1993 Papanek told the *Design Renaissance*, the world design congress in Scotland:

'What many of us are hoping for is a profound change in the way things look and work that is based on more than an arbitrarily invented style ... When design is nourished by a deep spiritual concern for environment, people and planet, this moral and ethical standpoint will provide the new forms and expressions – the new aesthetic – we are all desperately trying to find ... The rise of a new aesthetic that is formed by environmental and ecological considerations will be unpredictable in its shapes, forms, colours, textures and varieties, and – at the same time – enormously exciting.'

These words sum up the essence of John Makepeace's mission to encourage a new generation of designer-entrepreneurs at Parnham College and Hooke Park. Certainly the recent furniture from his own workshop, such as the Vine Chair and Standing Stones Table, reflects an aesthetic which

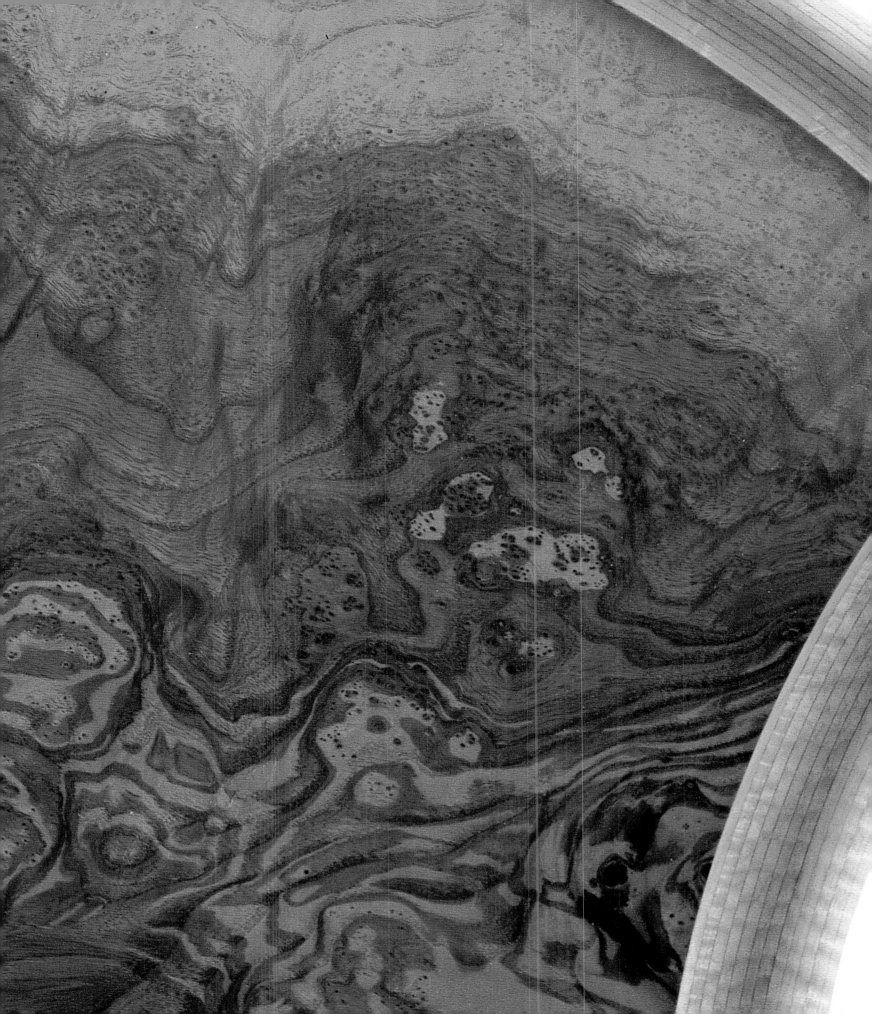

Corner of a table in sycamore and solid ash.
The natural grain of the material becomes the surface
pattern, requiring no additional application
of decoration.

is a very literal reading of ecological forms, but he regards this interpretation of the natural object as the first step towards a greater aesthetic exploration of abstraction in furniture design. 'I enjoy abstraction in modern art and sculpture, but it goes beyond the point which is directly achievable in furniture, where function plays such a significant role. However, it is likely I will go a lot further in the direction of the abstract in the future.'

Makepeace is acutely aware that the Modern Movement has taught us all to look more closely at forms, with the result that present-day furniture makers face a new and different challenge from those of the past: to create abstract sculpture. 'I now feel ready to address the conflict between Modernism and Expressionism in my own work', he says. One essential influence of Modern Movement thinking on Makepeace's approach can be seen in his growing interest in abstraction. In the past less has rarely been more in his work, and some critics have commented on the vulgarity of some of his ideas and the over-ornateness of some of his finishes. But the interrelationship of different elements is always clearly legible in his finest pieces, and his design influences reflect the value he places on the adoption of simple solutions to complex problems. When Sir Norman Foster's highly engineered black-and-steel Nomos Desking System was exhibited at Parnham, it was never as incongruous as the media's stereotypical image of Parnham – as a community of wood worshippers – might have suggested.

Meanwhile, the exploration of the organic forms of bio-architecture at Hooke Park can be seen as an extension of the potential of modern architecture rather than an abrupt counterblast to it. As Professor James Gordon comments on the contemporary efforts to unite biology and engineering: 'One requirement of innovative creativity is clearly to break away from the tyranny of tradition – which is what the Impressionist painters had to do. But if one breaks away from precedent, where is the imagination to browse? At least partly, I think, in the world of bio-mechanics where, even if there are no direct exemplars, both the technical and the artistic imagination are stimulated in a largely novel way.' The fusion of the technical and artistic imagination is where Makepeace's strengths lie.

VINE CHAIR

Handcarved in lime and painted by Adrian Everett, the Vine Chair represents John Makepeace's increasingly literal reading of ecological forms in his work. This is no ironic reference to the environment; instead, it is a direct and powerful evocation of the natural surroundings which have been such a sustaining creative influence throughout his career.

The frame and legs of the chair are conceived as rugged trunks. Fleshy leaves form the seat and back. The overt figurative quality of the detailing and colouring of the leaves (see left) goes against the grain of most contemporary furniture making. But Makepeace, who has never been afraid to put his head above the parapet and dodge critical blows to forge his own artistic path, is unapologetic. He believes that the vividness and unpredictability of natural colours and forms should be matched by a similar diversity of expression in furniture making.

By combining furniture making, woodcarving and painting in a single, holistic art form, he reinterprets the relationship between function and nature.

PHOENIX TABLE

Makepeace's preoccupation with environmental sustainability is not confined to his activities at Hooke Park. It can be viewed as a key artistic concern in recent work emanating from the Parnham workshop.

This breakfast table is an eloquent statement about the capacity of nature to renew itself despite Man's abuse of the earth's resources. Its base of burr oak is scorched, but out of it rises laminated oak legs (see left) which support a top of burr oak and holly, representing the canopy of the tree.

The piece is an essay about the forest as a sustainable source of material. It draws, says Makepeace, on the mythology of the phoenix rising from the ashes. This narrative and metaphorical style of designing objects, which are also perfectly functional, represents Makepeace's determination to extend the vocabulary of contemporary furniture and abandon the contraints of modern orthodoxy in design.

In autumn 1994 John Makepeace returned to Templeton College (formerly the Oxford Centre for Management Studies) to participate in an intensive residential management course and kindle the fires of his own creativity. Since this was the college that had provided the model for Parnham's own school, the return there to undergo a week of self-scrutiny was a significant one.

A personality test revealed Makepeace to be a 'theorist' – that is, someone who assimilates disparate facts and turns them into coherent theories, a perfectionist who will not rest easy until things fit into a rational scheme. That much he already knew. But another project proved far more self-revealing. The group was asked to design an organization which is dynamically unstable. The idea of dynamic instability derives from a technical concept employed in the aerospace industry in which flexible airborne structures use changing wind and air currents to propel themselves forward on their chosen course. Makepeace began to recognize its characteristics in his own activities. Dynamic instability is often accompanied by a single-minded determination to realize a vision at all costs. Its diametric opposite in business terms is inertia – a visionless approach in which one is driven in different directions by the market.

In the shape of Makepeace's career it is possible to see a gradual move towards dynamic instability. In the early years he was market-driven, especially during the 1960s, when he made retail products in volume by machine. But, once he began to focus on making furniture by hand, he was able to develop a single-minded vision and move towards a state of dynamic instability in which he could conduct his affairs in a spirit of adventure. The community at Parnham is beginning to thrive on this concept. In his speculative development of the Creation Collection in 1994 Makepeace showed a gambler's hand, taking more artistic risks than ever before in the hope of winning greater commercial and critical reward; this is perhaps the clearest manifestation yet of his dynamic instability.

Dynamic instability means never cashing in the chips and settling for the status quo. It means relentlessly surging forward to the next organizational and creative challenge. But such an approach clearly takes its toll on the man driving things into the wind. Makepeace has built a strong and supportive team around him, without whom he could not generate all the initiatives he does. However, he admits that he has had to be cavalier on occasions to force his ideas through, and behind him there is a history of bruised egos and fractured relationships of the kind which lie in the wake of any go-getting pioneer. He has very few close personal friends. Indeed, there is no domestic dimension to his life at all; even the fact that his home at Parnham House is open to the public twice a week is all part of the grand design to find the widest possible audience for his ideas. Many Parnham graduates have left the Plantagenet manor in Dorset remarking that they found it easy to respect the man but far harder to get to know and like him. Makepeace, unusually, combines the confidence and skills of a natural communicator, who attracts people readily to his ideas, with the remoteness of a driven personality dedicated to a life of self-sacrifice.

Detail of the carved lime Feather Chair: Makepeace is prepared to take risks to achieve wider artistic recognition.

Perhaps the most marked reflection of dynamic instability in the work of John Makepeace is also the most deep-rooted. It is apparent in the way in which he works with his professional craftsmen on the interpretation of his designs, a process that sheds valuable light on a contemporary debate in the crafts in Britain about the nature of skill.

This debate has been fired by a polemical thesis written by Peter Dormer entitled *The Art of the Maker*, in which the twentieth-century emphasis on self-expression and individuality in modern painting, sculpture and studio craft is attacked for the way in which it has undermined the value of practical skill, and has severed the links between craft knowledge and the fine arts. 'There is almost a degree of neurosis about being (and being seen to be) unique; about having something or being something inimitable', says Dormer. He quotes the American art critic Clement Greenberg as saying: 'Conception (intuition/inspiration) alone belongs to individuals; everything else, including skill, can now be acquired by anyone.' Faced with attitudes of this kind, Dormer argues, craft work has become misunderstood and neglected.

Makepeace has, however, made a conscious bridge between conceptual and craft-making skills in his approach and sees no conflict between the two. As an apprentice he was initially content to master materials and processes on a technical level, a mastery which is reward enough for many craftsmen. But he soon progressed to the acquisition of design skills in order to communicate with an audience, and eventually came to conceive of the designing of individual pieces of furniture as an art form. 'An artist sets a different bench-mark from a maker', he explains. 'A maker will want to get it right ten times out of ten. An artist has more elusive targets. One success out of ten will suffice, with the other nine pieces acting as sketches, prototypes and support material along the road to that significant artistic result.'

Part of Makepeace's success in turning craft skill into a key element of the conceptual process, and in pursuing the path of dynamic instability in all facets of his work, can be traced back to his decision in the mid-Seventies to give up making pieces in the workshop himself. 'I began to spend more time in different places with different people and that had an influence on my design thinking', he explains. 'I was not stuck at the bench. I was beginning to explore educational, environmental and economic issues and, as those interests grew into a new spectrum of activity, so I was able to feed them all back into my designing.'

It is clear that Makepeace has been able to view the making process more dispassionately by stepping back from it. In particular, he has been able to see how material, technique and function, instead of putting a brake on creativity and self-expression, can be the primary stimulus for them: 'I still get terribly excited about new pieces and I still endeavour to spend time with my craftsmen on an almost daily basis. But my approach now is to use the information coming to me via the making process to enhance the design of the object. It is hard to do that when you are making it yourself. If you are creating an individual piece, never to be replicated, it is important to respond all the time to what you are learning from the process of making it.'

Makepeace acknowledges that rarity by itself is not enough to confer value on a handmade object. Content and concept are important, and he has been conspicuously successful in creating a series of furniture pieces which underscore the entire ecological crusade at the centre of his life. The patrician idea of the artist-craftsman as someone who can turn philosophical values into tangible objects was never more true than it is of Makepeace.

Previous page: *Detail of the Phoenix 2 Chair.*

Below: *Adding the holly bullrushes to the Phoenix 2 Chair which has a burr elm seat and bog oak legs. Makepeace has been able to view the making process more dispassionately by stepping back from it.*

Right: *The two-seater Embrace Bench, made entirely of hickory sourced from Kew following the storms which raged across southern England in 1987, tearing down trees. Function, technique and material are a spur to creativity, not a brake, according to Makepeace.*

196

Throughout history there have been landmark design studios which have produced furniture of exceptional quality. Whether this has been due to the patronage of kings or to the adoption of new technologies, certain designers have been destined to make their mark. Makepeace believes that his name will have a place in that history, and it deserves to. 'I have a curious sense of destiny about my work', he meditates. 'Every piece of my furniture reflects an ethos about our environment – it signals a particular time, a place and an approach.' Though the remote rural setting for the pursuit of his vision might have been drawn from the manuscript of a medieval craft guild, the ethos that sustains the work of John Makepeace will not be out of place in the twenty-first century.

Steamer chairs in beech with cotton fabric: craft objects of value will have their place in the sun in the next century, believes John Makepeace.

Acknowledgments

AUTHOR'S ACKNOWLEDGMENTS

The achievements featured in this book bear witness to the outstanding support and generosity of the many friends, Patrons, Donors and Trustees who have shared, encouraged and guided my endeavours over the last thirty years. To them I extend my heartfelt tribute of appreciation and respect.

John Makepeace

The Iliffe Family Charitable Trust
The Interbuild Fund
John Keil Ltd
The John S. Cohen Foundation
E.D. Jowett
A. Kirkup
L .G. Harris & Co Ltd
Dr P. Laight
D. and G. Langton
Sir Geoffrey Leigh
The Lloyds Bank Charitable Trust
Lloyds Bank plc
The Lloyds Bowmaker Group
Lloyds, Members and Brokers
Loders Garage
London & Manchester
Assurance plc
Lord Clinton's Charitable
Settlement
Lord Farringdon's 2nd Charitable
Trust
The Mackintosh Foundation
Marks & Spencer Ltd
Marley plc
O.J.D. Marriot
E., J. and F. McAlpine
J. Mattison Ltd
Midland Bank plc
Mis A.E. Waley Cohens Charitable
Trust
Miss Hazel M. Woods Charitable
Trust
M. Montgomery
Moulton Developments Ltd
Norcross plc
Norman Adams Ltd
Sir David Ogilvy
Olivetti Ltd
The P.F. Charitable Trust
E.C. Packer
J. Parker
Sir Peter Parker
J.C. Peake
Penn Mill Motors
S.S. Plackett
The Portrack Charitable Trust
The Post Office
D.M. Print
Provincial Insurance plc
Sir John Quicke and family
The R.J. Harris Charitable Trust
The Rayne Foundation
Rentokil Group plc
Robert Fleming Holdings Ltd
The Robert McAlpine Foundation
The Robinson Charitable Trust
Rockwool Ltd
Rothmans International plc
The Roy Fletcher Charitable Trust
Royal Bank of Scotland plc
Rye Machinery

The S.H. Burton 1956 Charitable
Settlement
The Samuel Storey Family
Charitable Trust
T.M.S. Saouilli
Sarna UK Ltd
The Scottish Forestry Trust
Sherfield (Investments) Ltd
I.A. Simcha
The Smallpeice Trust
The South Square Trust
St Pier Ltd
J.J. Studzinski
The Swire Charitable Trust
S. Taylor
The Thornton Foundation
3i Trustee Group plc
Tregarne Agencies
Unilever plc
Viscount Amory Charitable Trust
Viscount Hood Settlement
W G I Ltd
W.H. Smith Group plc
M.B. Watson
Mrs A. Wheatley-Hubbard
G.H.H. Wheler
Whitbread plc
P.G.H. Wilson
Dr J. Wonham
J.D. Wood

The A.S. Butler Charitable Trust
Abbey National plc
A.C. Adams
C. Adams
Sir Adrian Cadbury
The Albert Reckitt Charitable Trust
Alcan Ltd
H. Alexander
Sir Lindsay and Lady Alexander
The Alsford Charitable Trust
Amey Roadstone Corporation
The Andrew Carnwath Charitable
Trust
The Antony Hornby Charitable
Trust
Arther Andersen & Co
The Ashendene Trust
The Hon Hugh Astor
The Marquess of Bath
BET plc
The Baldwin-Bewdley Trust
E. Balfour Brown
The Balney Charitable Trust
J.G.W. Bankes
P. Barter
Benn Brothers Ltd
The Benn Foundation
Capt G. Best
A.J. Binns
A.K. Birkett

J. Blewitt
Dr B.K. Blount
Blue Circle Industries plc
J. Blunt
W. Bordass
J. Botts
Bow Park Investments Co Ltd
K. Bradford
Broadlands
Prof B. Brooke
B. Broomfield
Burmah Oil
Sir Charles Cave
A. Cayzer
Sir James Cayzer
The Cazenove Charitable Trust
Cedar Antiques
P. Chappell
Christies plc
The Clifford Charity
G. Clifford
Lady Colfox
The Coutts Charitable Trust
M. Darton
D.T.H. Davenport
The De La Rue Jubilee Trust
G.R. Dorey
Dorset Food Products Ltd
The Marquess of Douro
G. Durrell
K.S. Dyson
The Earl of Bradford 1981
Charitable Trust
The Earl of Hareword's Charitable
Trust
The Earl of Shelburne's Charitable
Trust
P.B. Eastwood
C.C. Empson
Ernst & Whinney
The Evode Group plc
The Fagus Anstruther Memorial
Trust
Sir Leonard Figg
M. J. and F. Fisher
Forestry Investment Management
A.D.G. Fortescue
R.D.V. Garnett
O. Garsrud
George Sykes Ltd
The Goldsmiths' Company's
Charities
Greenwood Syndicate
Hamworthy Heating Ltd
H. J. Hann
Henry Venables Ltd
A. Hepburn-Scott
R. Heseltine
R.M. Hewitt
The Hoare Trustees
T. Holland-Bosworth

The Hon H.M.T. Gibson Charitable
Trust
The Hon Philip R. Smith Charitable
Trust
Sir Simon Hornby
J.E. Hubbard
F. Hummel
T. Huxley
The I.J. Lyons Charitable Trust
Idlewild Trust
N. Illingworth
The Ingleborough Estate
Ionian Bank Ltd
D.J. Ironside
The J.M. Simpson Charitable
Settlement
J.M. Stratton & Co
James Latham Ltd
N.D.G. James
F.O. Jayne
John Perring Ltd
H. Johnson
The Joicey Trust
Dr I. Kay
A.T. Klimacki
G. Kunzle
Z. Kurtz
The Lady Hind Trust
N.A.G. Laing
Lady Lane
Laverstoke Estates Ltd
Leconsfield Estate Company
N.P. Lister
Viscount Boyne
Lord O'Neill's Charitable
Settlement
The Loseley & Guildway Charitable
Trust
The M.T.N.H. Wills 1962 Charitable
Trust
The Marlborough Charitable Trust
Marples Ridgeway, Sheffield
T. Martys
M. McIntyre-Reed
Memory of Ronald Fryer Dickenson
The Mills Charity
Sir Jasper Moore
S. Mornay
Mrs Greenwood's Settlement
of 1.4.1996
The Nancy Balfour Trust
S.J.G. Neal
J.K. Nicholson
Sir Arthur Norman
The Marquess of Northampton
The Duke of Northumberland
The Odgers family
Sir Duncan Oppenheim
A.D. Owen
T. Palmer
W.H.M. Papworth

N. Partridge
J. Pattinson
J.A. Payton
Perring Furnishings
The Peter Mayer Charitable Trust
The Peter Ward Charitable Trust
Pitt Rivers Charity
N.J.E. Pluck
The Earl of Plymouth
Powell & Robinson
The R.H. Harris Charitable Trust
The Royal Society for the
    Protection of Birds
The Radcliffe Trust
Radford Ltd
The Radnor Charitable Foundation
K. Rankin
The Red How Charitable Trust
The Redmayne Charitable Trust
Sir Patrick Redmayne
Cosmo Rodewald
Lord Romsey
The Earl of Ronaldshay
Rowe & Pitman
S.J. Bootle Wilbraham
The Schroder Charity Trust
Securicor Group plc
Sedgewick Group plc
P.F. Seebohm
Sir Andrew Carnwarth's Charitable
    Trust
Sir E.C. Bacon's Settlement
Sir Richard Carew-Pole's 1973
Charitable Trust
SIS Ltd
M. Skan
Slough Estates plc
Solent Furniture
Lady Solti
The Duke of Somerset
Somerton Erleigh Estate
Sotheby Parke Bernet & Co
Southern Television
Spur Shelving Ltd
Standard Chartered Bank Ltd
Stobart & Sons
L.G. Stopford Sackville
R. Sturdy
The Tanglewood Trust
The Taylor Woodrow Charitable
    Trust
Thames Television
The Hon M.L. Astor's 1969
Charitable Trust
Mrs Joan Leach 14th Trust
Thomas Tilling plc
The Thoresby Charitable Trust
The Timothy Coleman Charitable
    Trust
Trafalgar House plc
Travis Perkins plc
The Turner Trust

M.B. Unthank
The Van Neste Foundation
M.K. Van
The Vernon Charitable Trust
Lord Vinson
S.M. White
E. Wolf
V.A.E. Wood
Col J. Woodhouse
P.J. Woods
The Worshipful Company
    of Turners
J.G. Wyatt
The Earl of Yarborough
M. Yates

PUBLISHER'S ACKNOWLEDGMENTS

The Publishers would like to thank Nicholas Jones (Reed Corporate Relations), Caroline Ducie and Susan Beale (Parnham) for their help in the production of the book.

PICTURE ACKNOWLEDGMENTS

The author and publisher thank the following photographers and organisations for their kind permission to reproduce the following photographs:

John Makepeace Archive 22, 23, 28-30, 92-93
Photograph: Theo Bergström 19- 20, 24 -25
Photograph: Peter Cook/Architects: AB+K 150-151
Photograph: Mike Murless, Farquharson & Murless 8, 11, 15, 17, 18, 26, 34-36,
    39-49, 61-63, 74 -75, 90, 95, 96 above, 97-99, 101-103, 105, 106 right, 108, 109,
    113, 114 -115, 117-121, 130, 134, 140-143, 159, 176, 178, 180-187, 190, 191,
    194 -195, 197-199
Photograph: Mike Murless, Farquharson & Murless/
    Illustrations: Shona Mackie 174-175
Photograph: Mike Murless, Farquharson & Murless/Designer: John Souter 72
Photograph: Paul Lipscombe 56
Photograph: Jonathan Lovekin 123-129, 131, 132, 135, 138, 139, 188-189, 192-193;
Photograph: John Makepeace 21
Photograph: Mann and Man 2
Photograph: Mann and Man/Designer: Jeremy Choppen 71
Photograph: Michael Nicholson 37-38
Photograph: Philip Partridge 12; /Photograph: Lisa Siegelman 32
Photograph: Michael Tropea 136-137
Photograph: Jeremy Whitaker 53
Photograph: George Wright 6, 59, 66, 69, 94, 196.
Hooke Park/Photograph: Nigel Gilbert/Designer: John Russell-Sanders 170
Photograph: Mike Murless, Farquharson & Murless 144, 147, 153-157/
    Designer: Claire Richter 171.
Parnham Archive (Courtesy of Cyril Poole) 54, 55, 58.
Parnham College/Photograph: Douglas Cape/Designer: Florian Harmer 73
Photograph: Mann and Man/Designer: Hans Christian Usadel 76
Designer: Brian Reid 77
Designer: Esther Hall 78, /Designer: Keith Lobban 79.

Richard Bryant/Arcaid 111
Paul Rafety/Arcaid 116
Designer: Christian Gaze for Gaze Burvill 168-169
Photograph: Peter Cook/Architects: AB+K 149
Edward Cullinan Architects 160, 162-163
Fiell International Ltd. 106 left, 107, 110
Photograph: Ken Adlard/Conran Octopus/Designer: Nina Moeller 86,
Photograph: Ken Adlard/Conran Octopus 96 centre and below, 100,
    114 left, 122 left, 202
Photograph/Designer: Robert Kilvington 89
Courtesy of David Linley Furniture 80
Photograph/Designer: James M. Marston 172
Clive Nichols 50, 68
Photograph: Graham Pearson/Designer: Nicholas Pryke 84-85
Designer: Roy Tam/Trannon Furniture 165
Photograph: Mike Murless, Farquharson & Murless/Designer: Petter Southall 173
Designer: Malcolm Strong 166-167
Photograph: Mike Helmsley, Walter Gardiner Photography/
    Designers: Wales & Wales; 81-83
Reproduced courtesy of the Trustees of the Wallace Collection 104
Photograph: Jeremy Whitaker 57
Photograph: George Wright 64-65

Index of Makepeace Furniture Designs

Numbers refer to pages on which the complete piece is illustrated

Index

Page numbers in *italic* refer to illustrations